Close Enough to Care

Pat Springle

Close Enough to Care

Rapha Publishing/Word, Inc.
Houston and Dallas, TX

Close Enough to Care,
Helping a Friend or Relative Overcome Codependency
by Pat Springle

Copyright © 1990
Rapha Publishing/Word, Inc.
Houston and Dallas, TX

First Printing, 1990

ISBN: 0-945276-18-4
Printed in the United States of America

To Mark, Robert, Hub, Jim, and Joyce . . . for helping me.

Contents

Acknowledgments

I want to thank the following people for their contribution to this book. Many thanks to . . .

- Sandy Ballard for typesetting my chicken scratch again!

- Jim Walter, Mark Baker, Richard Price, and Matt Barnhill for reading the manuscript and giving me valuable advice.

- Stan and Pam Campbell for editing the book to eliminate and take out lots of the many redundancies. (I didn't send them this part!)

- Joey Paul and the folks at Word, Inc. for publishing this book with us, and

- Robert S. McGee for his desire to help individuals and entire families experience the restoration and refreshment that Christ can give.

Foreword

After I read Pat's first book, *Codependency* (Rapha Publishing/Word, Inc.), I realized that there are literally millions of people who need help if they are going to overcome their problems with codependency. So, I asked Pat to write this book for the friends or relatives of codependents. Strained relationships have created the problems of codependency. In contrast, nurturing relationships play an important role in the healing process.

Many people are confused about the use of the word *codependency*. As Pat explains in *Close Enough to Care*, the term comes from work with the families of alcoholics in the 1970s. The alcoholics were "dependent" on alcohol, and their families were regarded as "codependents" because they exhibited dysfunctional patterns of rescuing, denial, shame, and control in their relationships with the alcoholics. The term *codependency* has subsequently been used when referring to individuals who are affected by families where substance abuse, addictions, divorce, and other dysfunctional behavior is present.

Codependency is a very real problem in our culture. Counselors and therapists are very familiar with such cases and the consequences. Others, however, are new to the problems of codependency. The varied theories and approaches to recovery can be quite confusing to these "helpers."

Though *Close Enough to Care* has been written to provide insights for helping or treating people who are codependent, the first part of the book will be especially helpful for those who are just beginning to learn about the complex emotional, spiritual, and relational problems which comprise codependency.

We at Rapha are glad to endorse this book as a very helpful tool for the person who wants to help a friend or relative conquer codependency.

Robert S. McGee
June 10, 1990

Chapter 1

The Codependent in Your Life

Will and Janice invited me to join them for dinner. Will and I had talked a couple of weeks earlier about his painful relationship with his parents. He now wanted to continue that discussion, this time with Janice present. Over spaghetti and salad, we again talked about his hurts and fears. He described his tremendous sense of responsibility to make his parents—especially his father—happy. He said he would do *anything* to get his father to love him.

After dessert, our discussion turned to the progress Will was making in his ability to be honest about his fears, hurts, and anger. He said, "I'm much more in touch with my anger..." then his voice became more somber as he continued, "but sometimes I blow up at Janice. How can I be honest about my anger and not hurt her?"

I looked over at Janice. She had obviously been deeply hurt by Will's outbursts. She looked confused as she asked, "What can I do to help him?"

~

Millions of people are in relationships with friends or family members who struggle with codependency. Like Janice, these people want to help, but most don't know how. Instead of helping, many of these people become victims of the codependent's behavior. They feel confused, hurt, and angry.

How about you? Is someone else's problem having a harmful effect on your life? In some of your closest relationships, do you feel confusion? Anger? Hurt? Determination? Hope? Numbness? Maybe you don't even have any idea why you feel these things.

Be assured that help is available for the person you love—and for you as well, but first you need a little background to see why the problems exist.

What is Codependency?

Codependency is a term coined in the 1970s in the context of treating alcoholism. Alcoholics were observed to share a somewhat consistent set of behaviors. As therapists treated families of these alcoholics, they noticed that the family members also exhibited a fairly consistent pattern of behavior. The alcoholic was *dependent* on alcohol. And since the family was affected, too, they were called *codependent*.

Later the term was given to families of those who were dependent on *any* kind of drug, including alcohol. Today the word is used to describe anyone in a significant relationship with a person who exhibits any kind of dependency. Some such dependencies are more subtle than others, and may include alcohol, drugs, sex, food, work, gambling, perfectionism, success, etc. The dependent person either consciously or unconsciously deprives others of needed love and attention. Codependents are people who are adversely affected by the dependent person's behavior. They typically have an imbalanced sense of responsibility to rescue, fix, and/or help the dependent person for the purpose of obtaining affirmation.

There are many definitions of codependency. In her best-selling book, *Codependent No More* (Harper and Row/Hazeldon), Melody Beattie defines a codependent person as, "one who has let another person's behavior affect him or her, and who is obsessed with controlling that person's behavior." Another definition of codependency is:

Preoccupation and extreme dependence (emotionally, socially, and sometimes physically) on a person or object. Eventually, this dependence on another person becomes a pathological condition that affects the codependent in all other relationships. This may include...all persons who (1) are in a love or marriage relationship with an alcoholic; (2) have one or more alcoholic parents or grandparents; or (3) grew up in an emotionally repressive family....It is a primary disease and a disease within every member of an alcoholic family."[1]

Simply put, and for the purposes of this book, codependency is *a compulsion to control and rescue others by fixing their problems.* It occurs when a person's God-given needs for love and security become blocked in a relationship with a dysfunctional person, resulting in three primary characteristics: a lack of objectivity, a warped sense of responsibility, and being controlled by and controlling others. Codependency is also manifested in three corollary characteristics: hurt and anger, guilt and loneliness. The codependent's every relationship and desire is affected. His goal in life is to avoid the pain of being unloved and to find ways to prove that he is lovable. It is a desperate quest.[2]

Some people define codependency quite broadly and they assert that almost any relational problem or desire to please people is a sign of codependency. They suggest that 98% of the population is codependent. But such a definition makes the term fairly meaningless. The problem is more specific. Codependency is a *compulsion* to control and rescue others, a sense of *having to* get others' approval at all cost, and a *need* to control the emotions, attitudes, and behaviors of others. Still, even with the more narrow definition, there are a lot of codependents! Speaking of the millions of alcoholics and their families in this country, Dr. Joseph A. Pursch of the Family Care Clinic in Santa Ana Heights, California, observed, "We know that the average affected family consists of 1.8 alcoholics/addicts and four codependents."

Children from divorced homes often develop codependent characteristics. In her article "Bouncing Back Slowly," Judith S. Wallerstein asserts that caretaking by "overburdened" children probably "runs much higher than the 15 percent we saw in our study."[3] And when we consider other dysfunctional homes where there is drug addiction, workaholism, eating disorders, sexual disorders, absent father or mother, and a variety of verbal, physical, and emotional abuses, we can see that codependency is a widespread problem in our society.

Codependents need help, and there are many available resources to aid them in identifying and dealing with their problems (including my own book, *Codependency*, Rapha Publishing/Word, Inc.). But another large group of people need help as well—the friends and family of codependents. The intent of *this* book is to equip that group of people to recognize codependency and be of assistance to those who suffer from its symptoms.

Why Do Those in a Relationship with a Codependent Need Help?

A relative, friend, or employer of a codependent needs help because codependency can be so confusing, frustrating, and difficult to understand. A codependent may behave in strange ways, including:

- feeling responsible for *your* behavior, but not for his own.
- intensely needing to be needed.
- expecting you to make him happy.
- being demanding or indecisive.
- being attentive and caring one minute, and selfish and cruel the next.
- seeing people and situations as wonderful or awful, black or white, with no shades of gray.
- overreacting to people or situations he can't control.
- seeking affirmation and attention, or sulking and hiding.
- believing himself to be perceptive, yet denying the obvious problems in his own life.
- seeing others as being "for him" or "against him."
- getting hurt very easily.
- using self-pity and/or anger to manipulate others.
- feeling like he/she needs to rescue people from themselves.
- communicating contrasting messages, like, "I need you. I hate you."
- not saying what he/she means, and possibly not meaning what he/she says.
- being deeply repentant, but doing the same thing again and again.

No wonder the friends of such people become confused, hurt, and angry! Examples are legion. Fran's husband is from an alcoholic home. He is overly responsible, very attentive, and affectionate. She enjoys the fact that she can always count on him to perceive what she needs and to meet those needs, but he seems so tied to the approval of his parents. In fact, when he visits them, his savior tendencies toward his parents become consuming. "As soon as we drive into their driveway, he stops being my husband and becomes their little boy!" Fran exclaimed.

A friend of mine works with a woman who is a "rescuer." Tracy's father is a workaholic and was very demanding of her and her sister. Her sister became religious and irresponsible, and then dropped out of school. Tracy, however, tried desperately to win her father's love as she grew up. Now in her mid 40's, she is a diligent and faithful employee. She takes pride in her excellent work, but she is tense, rigid, and demanding with others around her. In any kind of dispute, she feels that she *can't* be wrong. The benefits of her superresponsibility are more than offset by the high level of tension in the office. My friend remarked, "She's always giving advice, even when she isn't asked. And she tries to control everybody's work. In fact, she sometimes does somebody else's work before they get to it. Some people in the office think she hung the moon. Others wish she would take up permanent residence *on* the moon! What am I going to do with her? I don't know whether to promote her or fire her!"

Trish is a young woman who told me that her mother is manipulative, but her father is passive. She described seemingly countless situations when her mother would communicate love and warmth but then use Trish's desire to please to control her. She was possessive. She believed no one else knew what was best for Trish (including Trish). As Trish explained all this to me, she said in an exasperated tone of voice, "I'm 27 years old, but mother treats me like I'm a five-year-old. She won't let me make my own decisions, and she even tries to tell me how to *feel*! I know she loves me, but sometimes she can be so insensitive and hateful toward me. She does so much for me, but I wish she'd stop and let me live my own life!" After a long pause, Trish said in a low voice, "Sometimes I just *hate* her...but I need to do what she wants because she's my mother. I am *so* confused."

Todd's friend, Phil, grew up in a home where there was no apparent addictive behavior, but a lot of condemnation and unmet needs. Phil's father gave him very little affirmation. Nothing Phil did was good enough for him, and he would often berate Phil for even the slightest mistakes. Phil's mother endured the same treatment from his father. She was a needy woman who desperately wanted to be understood and loved by *somebody*. She turned to Phil for emotional support. He described his relationship with his mother: "Even when I was in grade school, Mother would sit and talk with me for hours after school before Dad came home. She asked for my advice on everything, and when I told her what I thought, she'd say things like, 'Phil, *nobody* could *ever* understand me the way you do! And your advice is exactly what I need!' I grew up believing that I could solve every problem and right every wrong! In high school I started dating, but now, fifteen years later, I realize that the only women I date are ones who are incredibly needy. They need me, and I can talk to them about the deepest hurts in their lives, but after a while, I can't stand them! Then I move on to another needy woman." Todd asked me, "How do you help somebody like Phil? Where do I start?"

A Perspective on Christian Psychology

People who are in a relationship with a codependent person need help. They need insight into the problem, wisdom in how to treat the person, and encouragement to keep going when the codependent doesn't understand or appreciate the help. Help is available from two areas: Christian faith and psychology. As these two influences come together, they can provide much-needed relief for someone closely involved with a codependent person.

The field of Christian psychology—helping people deal with the realities of emotional, relational, and spiritual pain in their lives from a sound biblical perspective—has come a long way in the past few years. Some people, however, still consider the term *Christian psychology* to be an oxymoron—two mutually exclusive terms put together. This perception may be based on the opinions of a few people who have either failed to be objective about the reality of pain, or have failed to be soundly biblical in their approach. It is obviously a mistake to lump all Christian psychology together. Not all of it is bad, and not all of it is good. Each varies to some degree in its approach and effectiveness.

One helpful way to define Christian psychology is as "in-depth discipleship." Its goal is to help people relate to God and others in productive and healthy ways. It is an integral part of the Great Commission, enabling men and women to be freed up from emotional, relational, and spiritual shackles so they can love and serve Christ.

How can we know if a particular model of psychology is genuinely "Christian"? How can we determine if a school of thought blends accurate observations about the needs of people with the eternal truth of God's Word? We can examine three factors of any model which determine its validity: presuppositions, propositions, and processes.

Presuppositions examine the nature of man. Is he inherently good or sinful? How has God made him? How can man relate to God and to others?

Propositions define truth. What is truth? How do we know what is true? Is truth in the secular, natural realm as well as in the Scriptures? If so, how can we know whether a particular idea is truth or deception?

Processes describe change. What are the factors in growth? How do people change? Is it instantaneous or is it a slow process? Can it be both? What factors hinder growth? How can obstacles be overcome? How is truth understood and applied? What are the roles of the cognitive, relational, spiritual, character, and time factors in this process?

A central issue in determining whether a particular model of Christian psychology is soundly biblical is its perception of sin. Deep at the root of most problems is our rebellion or indifference toward God. We need to be honest about our sin and experience God's forgiveness, but for many of us, our own perceptions, relationships, desires, and hurts are immensely complicated and confused by the effects of others' sins, especially those of family members.

Becoming a Christian doesn't suddenly and completely wipe out all the effects of our sins or the sins of others. Sadly, our errant perceptions of Christianity have complicated and trivialized the way many of us deal with real issues in our lives. Instead of experiencing Christ's forgiveness, love, and strength, many of us only adopt higher ethical and behavioral standards for our lives. We live by more "ought's" and "should's" than ever before. Our defense mechanism of denial becomes stronger, not dissolved in the warmth and purpose of true fellowship with God and His people.

It is painfully ironic that some secular psychologists are often far more perceptive about emotional and relational problems than Christians are. In *Inside Out* (NavPress), Dr. Larry Crabb explains why Christians in our culture are often shallow and defensive about the deep needs in people's lives, being unable or unwilling to be objective about the complexity or depth of inner pain. Most of us hope that we won't have to deal with that sin after all. We expect God to somehow eradicate it if we will just do the right things or have enough faith.[4]

Our inability to adequately address the real issues under the surface of our lives is understandable for two reasons. First, we live in an instant society. We have instant banking, instant food, instant diets, instant news, and instant almost everything else. We have come to expect instant relationships and instant happiness. Long processes that examine unpleasant realities are not appealing to us.

The second reason is that in the last century, Christianity has been attacked by a variety of powerful forces—including higher criticism, Darwinism, and humanism—which have threatened its credibility. Many Christian thinkers have been preoccupied with defending the faith against these attacks instead of going deeper to apply the truth of the Scriptures in the context of the real needs in people's lives.

In the 16th and 17th centuries, the Puritans were called "physicians of the soul" because they presented authentic Christianity with real solutions and processes for real emotional, relational, and spiritual problems. We need a new tradition of modern Puritans who will be "physicians of the soul" in *our* culture and provide a powerful combination of the warmth of unconditional love, biblical truth, and patient processes. People must get below the shallow, instant answers and genuinely *experience* the grace and strength of God.

The Codependent and You

The codependent in your life may be at any given point in the process. He may have given you this book with a plea for help. He may be at the very beginning of the process, barely realizing that "something's not quite right in my life." He may be far down the road toward emotional health. He may not see the problem at all. He may accuse you of overreacting to his problems, and he may be hostile to any suggestions you want to make.

The codependent may or may not ever change, but *you* can! You cannot control another person's responses or choices. He has to learn to make his own decisions, acknowledge his own feelings, and be responsible for his own behavior. But you don't have to give in to his manipulation. You can be honest and healthy.

The goal of this book is the same one defined in 1 Timothy 1:5: *The goal of our instruction is love from a pure heart and a good conscience and a sincere faith.*

Our goal is love, not manipulation; from a pure heart, not absorbing dependence; a good conscience, not guilt, morbid introspection, or condemnation; and a sincere faith. It is hoped you will increasingly experience both intimacy and independence—for yourself and the codependent in your life.

By its nature, there are many complexities and variables in codependency. A person's background, personality, relationship with his parents, current relationships, immediate needs, and many other factors contribute to the mosaic of his or her life. There are no quick fixes and no simple formulas, but there *are* principles which will enable us to deal with the causes and the effects of codependency—and to get healthier ourselves. Also, these principles are foundational concepts that apply to a broad range of relational, emotional, and spiritual needs in people's lives. They are not limited to the realm of codependency.

This book is divided into three sections: Understanding Codependency, Understanding Yourself, and Facilitating the Healing Process. The next chapter provides a closer look at the nature of codependency, as well as its causes and consequences.

Summary

How would you define and describe codependency? Why do you think your friend or relative is a codependent? The following questions are taken from a helpful analysis of adult children of alcoholics, but they are applicable for all codependents. Answer the following questions with your friend or relative in mind:

1. Does he often feel isolated and afraid of people, especially authority figures?
2. Is he an approval-seeker, losing his own identity in the process?
3. Does he feel overly frightened of angry people and personal criticism?
4. Does he often feel that he is a victim in personal and career relationships?
5. Does he have an overdeveloped sense of responsibility, which makes it easier to be more concerned with others than with himself?
6. Is it hard for him to look at his own faults and his own responsibility to himself?
7. Does he feel guilty when he stands up for himself instead of giving in to others?
8. Is he addicted to excitement?
9. Does he confuse love with pity, and tend to love people he can pity and rescue?
10. Is it hard for him to feel or express feelings, including feelings such as joy or happiness?
11. Does he judge me or others harshly?
12. Does he have a low sense of self-esteem?
13. Does he often feel abandoned in the course of his relationships?
14. Does he tend to be a reactor instead of an initiator?

People who struggle with codependency usually have difficulties in many of these areas of their lives. All of us, of course, struggle with certain areas more than others, but these questions are designed to surface the major characteristics of codependency.

Describe your relationship with him or her. What are the strengths and weaknesses of the relationship?

Endnotes

[1] Sharon Wegscheider-Cruse, *Choicemaking* (Deerfield Beach, FL: Health Communications, 1985).

[2] Pat Springle, *Codependency*, 2nd ed. (Dallas, TX: Rapha Publishing/Word, Inc., 1990), pp. 23-24.

[3] Judith S. Wallerstein, "Bouncing Back Slowly," *New York Times*, Jan. 22, 1989.

[4] Dr. Larry Crabb, *Inside Out* (Colorado Springs, CO: NavPress, 1988) pp. 44-49.

Section 1

Understanding Codependency

This section contains excerpts from *Codependency* (Pat Springle, Rapha Publishing/Word, Inc.). For more depth on each of the aspects of codependency mentioned in Section 1, we recommend that you read this book.

Chapter 2

How Does a Person Become a Codependent?

When Richard started dating Betty, he could tell that she was a girl who knew how to have a good time! She was the life of the party. Sometimes she drank a little too much, but he'd say, "That's just Betty. She'll be all right." After they got married, life sailed along for a while, but Betty's drinking began to be a problem. She started drinking martinis at lunch and a couple of margaritas after work. "It helps me relax," she explained.

When she felt bad and didn't get the house cleaned up, Richard did it for her. When she was hung over and couldn't go to work, she asked Richard to call and tell her boss that she was sick. The first few times this happened, Richard did these things with the rationale that it surely wouldn't happen again. But it did.

Betty's drinking got progressively worse, and Richard was giving excuses to friends, neighbors, bosses, and everyone else they knew to cover for her irresponsibility. He not only worked hard at his job, he also worked hard at home. He washed clothes, cleaned, cooked, and he made excuses for Betty.

Richard wanted to have children, and thought, *Maybe a child will help Betty. Maybe she will stop drinking and be okay.* Ashley was born after they had been married for five years, but instead of helping Betty to stop drinking and become more responsible, Richard was expected to do more. He had to be both a mother and a father to Ashley. He loved his wife and child, but he became tired and angered by their demands. Then he felt guilty for being angry at his little girl. Richard's life was a wreck!

When they were first married, Richard had rationalized Betty's problem, and had felt compassion for her. But now he was angry. He felt used and lonely, and yet he continued to help Betty and make excuses for her. And he felt sorry for himself, sorry that anyone as kind and thoughtful as he was could be so misunderstood and mistreated. He even thought about taking Ashley and leaving Betty, but he wondered, *Where would she go to find somebody like me to take care of her? What would she do without me? She needs me!* So Richard stayed. He continued to "rescue" Betty, he continued to be angry with her, and he continued to feel sorry for himself. Nothing changed. Ever.

Codependency is not a surface problem with a set of isolated feelings or behaviors. Consequently, superficial solutions don't help. A deep hurt or an unmet need for love and acceptance either numbs the codependent or drives him to accomplish goals so he can please people and win their approval. Codependent emotions and actions are designed to blunt pain and gain a desperately needed sense of worth. The problem with codependent behavior is that it yields only short-term solutions which ultimately cause more pain.[1]

God has a different plan—His desire is our stability and security. He wants us to experience His love, protection, and provision. Dysfunctional families, however, wreck God's plan and create the pain, numbness, drive, and defense mechanisms characterized by codependency.

God's Design for the Family

The Lord designed the family as the primary environment for us to experience His love and strength. The husband-wife relationship and the parent-child relationship are intended to be reflections and models of our relationship with God. The function (or dysfunction) of these relationships shapes each family member's view of his self-concept and of God.

The husband is instructed to cherish his wife, to take time to understand her, provide for her, enjoy her, and love her in the same way that Christ does for

His people (Ephesians 5:25-33; 1 Peter 3:7; Colossians 3:19; Proverbs 5:15-19). In response to this strong and tender love, the wife is to respect her husband, enjoy her relationship with him, and develop her own identity and skills as she helps to provide for the family's needs (Ephesians 5:22-33; 1 Peter 3:1-6; Colossians 3:18; Proverbs 31:10-31). The husband and wife are to be intimate partners with a common purpose, but with distinct identities and roles.

Most children flourish in this kind of loving and strong environment. In the family that follows God's design, children are highly valued (Psalms 127:3; Mark 9:36; 10:15). They receive compassion for their hurts and disappointments (Psalms 103:13), loving correction and discipline (Proverbs 13:24), forgiveness and acceptance (Luke 15:11-24), patient and persistent instruction (Deuteronomy 6:6-9), and understanding in the context of love and direction (Ephesians 6:4; Proverbs 22:6).

Consistent, loving discipline is tremendously important to the development of children. Without it, they have no boundaries, no clear sense of right and wrong, and they are forced either to discipline themselves or suffer the discipline of an authority who primarily wants to restrict their destructive behavior. Receiving loving discipline as a child prevents many personal and interpersonal difficulties throughout life.

Both parents have a role in providing this environment. Some people, however, think that the mother is supposed to be tender and the father is supposed to be tough, but this is an incorrect view of the separate parental roles under God's design. Both are to be tender and compassionate (Luke 15:4-24; Psalms 103:13; Genesis 25:28; Exodus 2; 1 Thessolonians 2:7, 11) and both are to be strong (Proverbs 13:24; 31:10-31; Ephesians 6:4). When both parents offer affirmation, warmth, comfort, attention, and time, the child believes he/she is a valuable, special person.

Dysfunctional Families

Strong and loving families are becoming rare in our culture. The insatiable thirst for personal success and self-indulgent pleasures distorts God's design for the family. Selfishness replaces unconditional love in both husband-wife and parent-child relationships. We value positions, possessions, and pleasure. Spouses and children who interfere with our pursuits are considered nuisances—so much so that divorce has grown to epidemic proportions. As a result, many families are *dysfunctional*; that is, they do not function in the way that God intended. They do not provide the security, love, and acceptance that all people so desperately need.

Some disagree, but most experts are convinced that divorce is hard on children. Children of divorce show signs of stress. They are more emotionally troubled. The fear of divorce affects their love lives. They are forced to act as adults while still in their pre-teens (e.g., assuming adult responsibilities, comforting and caring for their divorced parents, caring for younger children without adult supervision). When parents remarry, this stress is compounded due to the death of the dream that mom and dad will get back together.[2]

Divorce is only one type of family dysfunction that has devastating effects on spouses and children. Yet, in every dysfunctional family, there is both the presence of negative, pain-inducing characteristics and the corresponding absence of some positive, nurturing characteristics. Characteristics of dysfunctional families may include:

alcoholism	neglect
drug addiction	verbal abuse
workaholism	emotional abuse
divorce	physical abuse
eating disorders	sexual abuse
sexual disorders	domineering father/passive mother
absent father	domineering mother/passive father
absent mother	

When these pain-inducing characteristics are present, there is an absence of (or severe shortage of) the qualities that people need to become healthy and secure:

unconditional love	comfort
unconditional acceptance	honesty
forgiveness	objectivity
laughter	freedom to express emotions appropriately
fun	friendship
a sense of worth	attention
compassion	time to work and play together
affirmation	appropriate responsibility
loving correction	freedom to have your own opinion and identity

To the degree that the development of these positive characteristics is hindered, the family members are hindered in their spiritual, emotional, and relational well-being. Among the many maladies in dysfunctional families is the compulsion to rescue, fix, and control people and situations.

Obviously, no family is perfect, but perfection is not the goal of family relationships. Relationships that are real, genuine, and honest are far better than perfectionism. Isn't it far preferable to know you will be forgiven for any shortcomings rather than attempting to maintain a standard of perfection you *know* is impossible?

The painful consequences of dysfunctional behavior in families are many and varied.

- A young girl from an alcoholic home seeks the love and affection she never got from her parents by going from one lover to another. But her empty feeling inside remains.
- The wife of a drug addict tries desperately to help him by making excuses for him and getting a job because he wastes so much money on pills. She is furious, but she just smiles and says, "That's all right, honey. I don't mind."
- An executive pours his life into his job and gets promotion after promotion just to prove to his parents that he is worthy of their respect.

- An elderly widow, whose husband was addicted to prescription drugs and committed suicide, expects her children to provide for her every need. They do, but she still nags them constantly, and none of them are happy.
- A college student is called "spacy" because she never seems able to pay attention. No one realizes that she was sexually abused as a child. Her drive to fix her parents' shaken marriage has been coupled with an abject fear of her father. She continues to feel that she is repulsive and dirty, and has withdrawn from everyone around her in a defensive attempt to block the pain.
- A youth pastor is very disciplined in his personal life and expects (demands) the high school students involved in his program to be just as committed and disciplined as he is. He is often disappointed at their "immaturity and rebellion" for not doing all that he has asked them to do. He appears to be the epitome of confidence and security, but secretly he wonders if his mother was right. She told him a hundred times, "You won't amount to anything!"

Tragically, the painful consequences of dysfunctional families do not end with the children. These consequences will be duplicated in generation after generation (Exodus 20:5) until either the original offense is diluted, or until someone has the insight and the courage necessary to change the course of his family's history.

Family Systems of Behavior and Communication

Significant research has contributed to much of what we now know about family systems of behavior. For purposes of simplification, these systems are usually identified as the functional family and the dysfunctional family.

The functional family, or family which contributes to the overall growth and development of its members, certainly isn't perfect. It does, however, foster open, honest, loving communication. In this environment, both the parents and their children develop a strong sense of "self," or identity. They learn that they can trust, feel, and talk about many—if not all—the issues in their lives. The diagram on the following page illustrates a functional family system:

The Functional Family System*

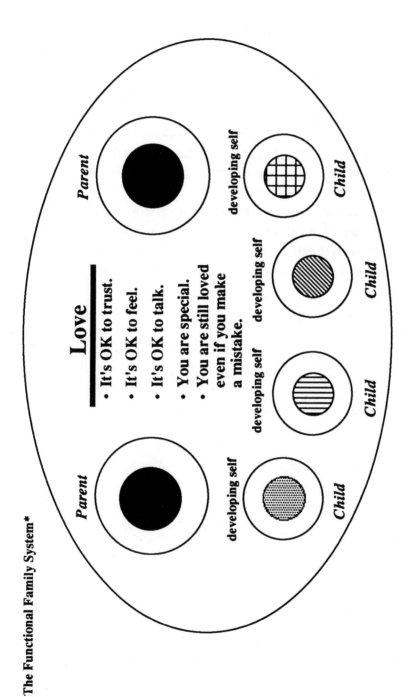

Parent

Parent

Love
- It's OK to trust.
- It's OK to feel.
- It's OK to talk.
- You are special.
- You are still loved
  even if you make
  a mistake.

developing self

developing self

developing self

developing self

Child

Child

Child

Child

In a dysfunctional family system, open, honest, loving communication is thwarted to some degree for any number of reasons. At least one person in the family is emotionally or physically abusive, absent, dependent, handicapped, physically or mentally ill, or manifests some other type of disorder. Resulting problems in family interaction may cause one or more members to feel that something is wrong, but negative communication systems hinder the freedom and ability to be honest about one's feelings. An unwillingness or inability to recognize problems in and around one's "self" promotes more repression and further erodes family trust and intimacy.

The diagram on the following page shows how dysfunctional family systems hinder trusting, feeling, and talking. The result is that each family member's growth and development is hindered, resulting in a loss of identity, or "self." Each person then takes one of several roles within the family often marked by codependent behavior.

The Dysfunctional Family System*

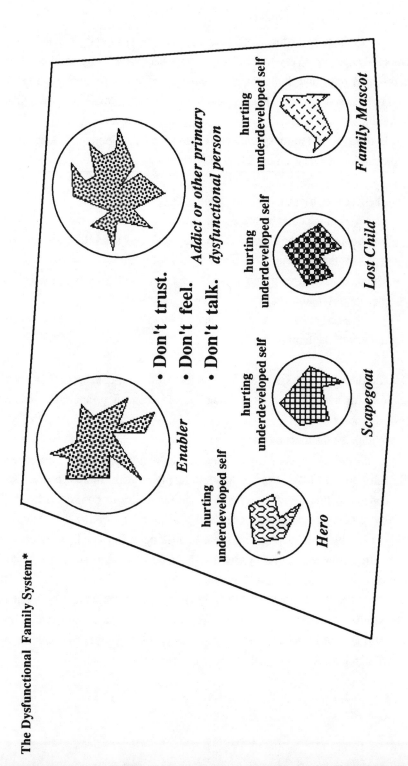

In the addictive/dysfunctional family system, the primary goal of the family members is survival. Very little development takes place in the children. They assume rigid roles and don't develop a strong sense of self-worth. As a result, they are doomed to keep playing these roles in their marriages and other relationships.

In this type of family system, most normal self-development is lost. All of the unconscious focus is on the addict or dysfunctional person.

- The **Enabler** tries to make everything OK.
- The **Hero** thinks that by being perfect the addition will go away.
- The **Scapegoat** rebels against the family problems and ultimately believes that *he* is the problem.
- The **Lost Child** pulls into a shell, withdraws, and isolates himself from meaningful relationships.
- The **Mascot** desperately tries to make everyone laugh in the midst of the tragedy of the family situation.

Children in these systems rarely build healthy self-concepts. They are at great risk for multiple marriages, addiction, codependency, and stress-related physical problems.[3]

Within the dysfunctional family system, some psychologists narrowly apply the term *codependent*. They say that the enabler is a codependent, but those in other roles are not. Many experts, however, apply the term more broadly. They have concluded that all of the people in the family try to control each other: some by rescuing, some by being successful, some by infuriating the rest of the family, some by withdrawing, and some by making others laugh. They control others' attitudes and behavior by pleasing them, making them proud or angry, or escaping from those attitudes and behaviors.

But what about rescuing? Certainly the enabler attempts to rescue others in the family. But the hero also tries to rescue others by calling attention to his successful accomplishments. The mascot tries to rescue people by soothing the pain through laughter. These roles are directly related to rescuing.

The scapegoat may have given up on rescuing, so he rebels from the sense of overresponsibility. The lost child, too, escapes from the burden of taking care of others by withdrawing into a shell. While these two roles do not exhibit rescuing tendencies, they do exemplify responses to the compulsion to rescue.

Roles often change within the family. One teenager changed from the hero of her family to the rebellious scapegoat when her sister changed from the scapegoat to the enabler. When one person changes, it often forces others to change their roles, too. But no matter what definitions are used to identify members of a dysfunctional family, each one needs to learn to experience an accurate perception of reality, love, and a sense of separateness.

The Need to Be Loved/The Need to Feel Valued

All people are created with a God-given need to be loved and to have a sense of worth. It is God's intent that these needs be met by two primary sources: (1) the grace of God through Christ, and (2) the reflection of His grace and strength in the family (and in the family of God). These two sources are not intended to function separately, but rather to form a cohesive environment. The content of the Gospel will have fertile soil when the character of God is modeled by the parents.

It is difficult to overestimate the influence of the family in a person's development. A child can grow up in a home with Christian parents who are too strict, critical, or neglectful. All types of dysfunctional attributes can exist in Christian families. The result will be a hurting, guilt-ridden, driven, overly responsible, or completely passive person. On the other hand, a child can be nurtured and protected in a home where the parents aren't believers. The warmth, affection, attention, and strength in this family will be much more likely to produce a stable and secure child than in a codependent Christian household. This may sound like heresy to some people, but children don't respond to theology. They care about being loved—really loved, not just in words but in deeds—with time, attention, and affection. They need time to relax, study, and play together. They need to be listened to and comforted when they hurt, and praised when they do well.

A person living in an environment of love and acceptance tends to blossom. But in dysfunctional families where these basic needs aren't met, people must seek other avenues to meet them. The compelling goal of their lives becomes having those needs met. Most of what they say or do is consciously or unconsciously designed to numb their pain, gain a sense of intimacy with others, and develop a sense of worth in their own eyes. Some escape to passivity. Some are driven to succeed as proof of their worth. Most do both in varying combinations.

Though codependency seems to serve our purposes of gaining control and approval, ultimately, it crushes our stability and our identity. It keeps us from enjoying all that God has for us. According to some psychiatrists and psychologists, the crushing nature of codependency most often does its awful work when people are most vulnerable—while they are young children. The eminent Harvard physician and child psychiatrist, Dr. Burton White, has found that during the first three years of a child's life, the home environment is critical. If those years are full of warmth, love, and protection, the child will probably develop a very healthy self-concept and view of life. If, however, a child grows up in a dysfunctional family, he will be deprived of these necessities to some degree, and his emotional and relational health will be adversely affected for the rest of his life. Dr. White does not take into account the power of God's Spirit to change lives, but his point is well taken: it is extremely difficult for a child to change his self-concept after the age of three![4]

Codependents long to be loved. They desperately want to have a sense of worth and specialness. Those needs are God-given, but in a dysfunctional family, the resources to meet those needs have often been withheld.

The Cause of Codependency

The following chart may help explain both the cause and the effects of codependency. The God-given needs for love, security, worth, protection, and provision are presented first. Then, two possible environments are contrasted with corresponding effects or consequences of each. The chart concludes with the motivational patterns that healthy and codependent people develop. Too

Needs	Environment	Results	Motivation
Love Security Worth	**Functional Family:** love, acceptance, forgiveness, protection, provision, honesty, freedom to feel, loving discipline	**Spiritual, emotional, relational health:** love, anger, fear, laughter, intimacy, willingness to take risks	**Healthy Motives:** love, thankfulness, obedience out of gratitude
Protection Provision	**Dysfunctional Family:** (alcoholism, drug abuse, eating disorders, etc.): condemnation, manipulation, neglect, abuse, unreality, denial	**Codependency:** lack of objectivity, warped sense of responsibility, controlled/controlling, guilt, hurt and anger, loneliness	**Compulsive Motives:** avoid pain, fear of rejection, fear of failure, gain a sense of worth, accomplish goals to win approval

often, we look at the behavior and emotions that result from codependency—either in ourselves or other people—and try to "fix" them without examining their cause. Hopefully, this chart will help you see a very clear cause.

Stages of Development

Many educators and psychologists have observed patterns in human development, from birth to adulthood. Some of these authorities explain this developmental process in minute detail, especially as it concerns infants. Others define it more broadly.

A basic understanding of the stages of human development can help us gain valuable insight into our emotional, relational, and spiritual progress—or lack of it. Four broad stages of development build upon one another. They are:

- Bonding (birth–two years old): the need to be loved.
- Separateness (two–eleven years old): the need to set personal boundaries, including what one is and isn't responsible for.
- Adolescence (twelve–eighteen years old): the need to develop adult relationships, gender behavior, and identity.

• Maturity (nineteen years of age and older): the need to continue growing in adult relationships, gender behavior, and identity.[5]

The ages given for each of the above stages are somewhat arbitrary because people develop at different rates for a wide variety of reasons. In fact, using only four stages to outline human development is a simplification of a very complex process. Each could be divided into many smaller, more defined stages which describe the subtle (and not-so-subtle) changes in a person's life as he grows and matures. Also, many aspects of development, such as bonding and separateness, are repeated again and again in different contexts and relationships throughout the growth process. The treatment of these stages here is only an introduction to the developmental process at the most rudimentary level. The basic concept, however, is that each stage serves as a foundation for the one after it.

Though the Scriptures do not outline stages of emotional, relational, and spiritual development in a systematic way, they do speak clearly and strongly about the needs that comprise these stages. For example:

• *Bonding*—Genesis 21:15-16; 1 Samuel 2:19; Psalms 103:13; 127:3-5; Isaiah 49:15; Mark 5:23; and Luke 2:48, among others.
• *Separateness*—Deuteronomy 6:6-9; Proverbs 22:6; 23:13-14.
• *Adolescence*—Psalms 119:9; 148:12-13; Proverbs 1:1-7:27 and many other passages.
• *Maturity*—Matthew 5-7; 10:5-42; 28:18-20.

A number of scriptural passages deal with adolescent and maturity issues such as values, choices, goals, motives, handling conflict, and spiritual warfare. Such passages are easier to understand and apply when one has developed a firm foundation of bonding and separateness. Though Scripture is for all of God's people and the distinctions between adolescence and maturity are often blurred, there does seem to be an observable connection between building a strong foundation of emotional, spiritual, and relational health and that person's free and full response to the Lord.

In this chapter, we will examine the stages when blockage stunts development and promotes codependent behavior: the stages of bonding and separateness. This chart gives an overview of the stages of development in regard to age:

Bonding: The Need to Be Loved

From birth to one-and-a-half or two years of age, a child's greatest need is to bond with his parents. Bonding means forming an attachment. Its purpose is to convey feelings of warmth, love, value, worth, closeness, trust, and specialness. Parents initiate this process by tenderly holding their baby, talking to him, making eye contact, playing with him, feeding him, changing his diapers and, generally, by giving him a lot of time and attention.

The father of a three-year-old girl had made a habit of holding her often and talking to her softly since she was an infant. One day, as he held her in his lap, he told her, "I love you, honey."

She looked up at him, smiled, and said, "I know that, Daddy."

"How do you know that?" he asked.

"Cause you tell me that all the time!" she replied.

Bonding—communicating warmth, affection, and value—takes time, attention and genuine love for the child. It can't be faked, and it can't be accomplished in a few hurried minutes from time to time. It is well worth the effort, however, because it forms a solid foundation for the second stage of development.

Separateness: The Need to Set Personal Boundaries

At about one-and-one-half years of age, a child learns a new word: "No!" He is learning to set limits and to assert his individuality. Bonding has to do with feeling loved. Separateness has to do with healthy independence. For the next ten years or so, the child learns to be comfortable with his thoughts and desires. He learns who he is and who he isn't. Here are some of the issues children begin to work through during this stage:

- I am responsible for this. I'm not responsible for that.
- This is what I feel. I don't feel that way.
- This is who I am. That is who you are.
- I am in control of my life. You are in control of your life.
- I believe this. I don't believe that.
- I want to be this way. You can be that way.
- I can see both sides of an argument. I don't have to be one-sided in my opinions.
- I make my own choices. You make your own choices.

It is during this second stage of development that the concept of one's "self" begins to emerge, laying the groundwork for the development of identity in later adolescence. If this budding concept of self is nourished and strengthened in a positive environment, a child will gradually learn to be perceptive, to think well, to experience (and express) his emotions and to relate to others.

Establishing boundaries during the stage of separateness is much like setting physical boundaries on a piece of property. The idea is that if each of us owned a ranch, we would individually be responsible for setting its boundaries, and then caring for it and protecting it. As caretakers, we also would be responsible for choosing whom to allow on our property. If invited to another person's ranch, we could visit, though we would not try to run anyone else's ranch, nor would we allow anyone else to run ours.[6]

In the same way, we have individual personalities (thoughts, feelings, and behavior), and we are responsible for setting our personal boundaries. We should establish what about ourselves we will share—and with whom. We may choose to allow certain others to share themselves with us. But we must avoid trying to run other people's lives, just as we should not allow others to run ours.

The desired result of the bonding and separateness stages is a healthy independence of one's self, not selfishness; a recognition of one's individuality, not isolation or self-indulgence.

A codependent person, however, doesn't "stay on his ranch." He goes over to others' ranches to farm the crops, live in the house, and tend the cattle. If the other person is needy, such as an alcoholic, he may at first welcome the intrusion of the overly responsible codependent. Others, however, may deeply resent this kind of meddling on their turf. And usually, even the addictive, needy people eventually resent the codependent's "help."

While he is taking care of someone else's ranch, the codependent neglects his own. He doesn't cultivate strength and stability in his own life because he's too busy strengthening others. He probably doesn't even realize his own ranch (his emotions, desires, behavior, attitudes, etc.) is being neglected. He only knows that he's doing the best he can do, and he sure hopes that other people appreciate his hard work and sacrifice for them.

Unfortunately, a number of us are still struggling with our individuality, our separateness from others. I recently had lunch with several couples. During the conversation, I asked one of the men what he thought about a program we were working on. He expressed his ideas articulately. Then I asked his wife for her opinions. Her ideas were very different from her husband's. After she finished, he spoke again, changing his opinions to fit his wife's.

I spent a few minutes with this man the next day and asked if he realized that he had changed his mind after his wife had expressed a dissenting opinion. He said, "Well, yeah. I guess I did."

"How often do you do that?" I asked him.

"Well...pretty often, I guess." This man was letting his wife's opinions and desires control him to a great degree. He had not learned to be separate, to have his own emotions, ideas, and behavior. He was letting her run his "ranch."

It isn't always easy to maintain a healthy sense of separateness from others. One young man I know was working on a committee for a civic club. Another person, a friend who was also on the committee, said to him, "Dan, the project we're working on is really important to me. I need you to stay late tonight and finish it."

Dan had told his wife that he would take her out to dinner that night. What would he do? How would he respond to his friend? Would he give in? And if he gave in, what would he say to his wife?

Dan was comfortable with his decision. He calmly replied, "I'm sorry, I can't stay tonight. I already have something important planned. If you could let me know a little sooner next time, I could probably work it out." Because he had learned to separate and to set limits as he was growing up, Dan was able to confidently express his decision to his friend.

The stages of bonding and separateness lay a strong foundation for the development of an adult identity in adolescence. However, if a person's development is blocked in these stages, codependent behavior—or even deeper issues—can result.

Deeper Issues

Academically, codependency is a subset of the problems that can occur in the separateness stage. Many codependents wrestle with more fundamental emotional and relational problems, problems in the bonding stage.

We have seen that healthy bonding between a child and his parents allows the child to develop a sense of worth and security. If there is unhealthy bonding or no bonding, this sense of value and love does not develop. Among the many and tragic symptoms of unhealthy bonding are: shame, self-hatred, emptiness, and the fear of closeness in relationships. The three corollary characteristics in our definition of codependency (anger, guilt, and loneliness) reflect the possibility of these bonding problems.

One of the main reasons people stay mired in the same problems year after painful year is that they simply do not recognize them as problems. They may see a few peripheral symptoms, but they tend to see themselves and their families as "normal." Parental modeling and family structure are powerful and lasting influences because children tend to believe that their parents are always right. Objectivity is a rare commodity, especially for someone who struggles with both bonding and codependency problems.

Denial, Rescuing, and Control

Though codependency is not limited to addictive environments, rescuing tends to surface more in addictive families (not just alcoholism and drug abuse, but also addictions to gambling, sex, work, success, food, etc.). People in such homes more obviously need to be rescued by someone. The act of rescuing is applauded, and is therefore reinforced. The failure to rescue is condemned, thereby manipulating the person to rescue next time...and the next.

Also, members of these families seem unaware of the addiction that is so destructive in the family. One researcher estimated that almost half of adult children of alcoholics deny a parental drinking problem, and 90% who *also* became chemically dependent could not identify any drinking problem with their parents.[7] Clearly, this dearth of awareness blinds family members to the reality of the problem, focuses the blame on themselves, and perpetuates both codependency and chemical dependency.

Codependents often act arrogant and demanding, but this behavior covers the fact that they are deeply hurting people. Their arrogance and condemnation of others is the way they defend themselves. When they fail, they blame others because they want to avoid the intense feelings of shame for their failure. One man spoke of his codependent wife, "She drives me crazy the way she rationalizes all the time! Why can't she just admit it when she fails?" The reason she has difficulty admitting her failures is that she feels intense self-hatred, shame, fear of rejection, fear of failure, and morbid introspection. She feels she simply can't stand any more, so she denies and rationalizes her problem.

Codependents are servants, but their servanthood has gone too far. They focus on the needs of others and neglect their own needs. They rescue and help others to feel appreciated. Rescuing is not a sincere desire to help from a foundation of strength and stability, but rather a compulsion to meet their own emotional needs.

An addictive or dysfunctional household is out of control, and the more out of control it seems to be, the more the codependent is compelled to control it. Control becomes an obsession. The codependent wants people to act, feel, and think a certain way (which is subject to change!) and he uses praise, neglect, sarcasm, affection, and any other means to keep people in line. He may be blind to the deeper realities in life, but he may be uncannily perceptive in his ability to "read" other people. He is likely to know exactly what to say or do to control and change the other person's feelings and behavior.

He may use niceness as a means to get people to be kind to him. A person who has been deeply hurt may develop into a very gentle and delicate person so others won't be harsh again, and tends to withdraw when hurt (which is fairly often).

In the environment of control, rescuing, denial, hurt and anger, codependents learn three rules about life: Don't trust. Don't feel. Don't talk. With little opportunity to work through the deep pain and anger that develops in these families, he becomes enmeshed in the lives of others, taking on their feelings, beliefs, goals, and values while losing his own in the process. He becomes dependent on the happiness and approval of people who are addictive or self-absorbed—the very people who can't meet his needs for love and acceptance. And he may follow the pattern of the addicted person, trying to numb the pain and develop some false sense of self-respect through drugs, alcohol, success, sex, gambling, or whatever else promises to work for him. He may become severely depressed because he has turned his intense anger inward for so long. Or he may simply continue to deny, rescue, and control.

Note: It is recommended that your friend or relative get a copy of *Codependency* (Pat Springle, Rapha Publishing/Word, Inc.), so he can begin to reflect on the issues in this section. You can finish this book while he is working through that one. Then, at whatever point he is ready to discuss his needs with you, you will be ready to discuss them. Also, you may want to get a copy of the book and work through the discussion questions at the end of each chapter.

Summary

1. What are characteristics of a functional family?

2. What are characteristics of a dysfunctional family?

3. What role does (did) your friend or relative play in his family? How did he act out that role?

4. In what stage was his development blocked? How can you tell?

5. Write your own definition for *codependency*:

Endnotes

[1] Pat Springle, *Codependency,* 2nd ed. (Dallas, TX: Rapha Publishing/Word Inc., 1990), pp. 5-6, 13.

[2] Anthony M. Casale, *USA Today, Tracking Tomorrow's Trends,* (Kansas City: Andrews, McMeel, and Parker, 1986), p. 111. See also Beth Brophy, "Children Under Stress," *U.S. News & World Report,* (27 October 1986), p. 63.

[3] Adapted from *The Family Trap* by Sharon Wegschieder-Cruse.

[4] Burton White, *The First Three Years of Life,* rev. ed. (New York: Prentice-Hall Press, 1985), pp. 323-4.

[5] Adapted from *Your Parents and You* by Robert McGee, Jim Craddock, and Pat Springle, (Dallas, TX: Rapha Publishing/Word, Inc., 1990) p. 29.

[6] Springle, *Codependency,* (pp. 192-3).

[7] Nicholi Armand, "Changes in the American Family: Their Impact on Individual Development and on Society," *Family Research Council,* p. 2. Reprint.

Chapter 3

The Primary Characteristics of Codependency

If we are to help a friend, spouse, or someone else through the often long and painful process of overcoming his codependency, we need to clearly understand what is going on in the mind, heart, and behavior of the codependent. First we will take a look at three primary characteristics the person is likely to exhibit: lack of objectivity, a warped sense of responsibility, and control.

Lack of Objectivity

Ken asked me have lunch with him and his wife, Helen. As we talked, Ken said that Helen had been feeling guilty and depressed since their previous visit with her parents. She explained, "Our last time with my parents was hard. My mother was very critical of me, and even of our children. I've felt really guilty since we left there."

"Tell me about your parents," I probed.

"My father is a wonderful man. He's loving and very supportive of me. My mother does a lot for me. She's very protective, but sometimes she can be kind of critical."

"Sometimes?" Ken looked at Helen.

"Okay, more than sometimes."

I asked, "What has your mother been critical of?"

Helen thought, and looked away as she answered, "When I was growing up, she criticized how I looked, the clothes I wore, my friends, and my grades. Now she's critical of my husband, my children...just about everything."

"How does your father respond when your mother criticizes you?"

"Oh, he goes into the living room and reads the paper. That's the way he copes when she nags him—which is just about all the time." She smiled weakly. "Daddy spends a lot of time in the living room reading the paper."

"How do you respond to your mother, Helen?"

"Well, I've always tried to make her happy. I've always wanted to please her, but I guess I just haven't been the daughter she wants me to be. I've really tried, though." Her voice trailed off.

"Helen, how *did* you, or how *do* you feel when your mother criticizes you?"

"Well, guilty, I guess...guilty that I can't make her happy, that I've failed as her child."

"How does she treat your children?"

"Just like she treats me. Her criticism has never bothered me, but I don't want her to treat my children that way! I just don't know how to get her to treat us well." Her voice was trailing off again as she looked down.

I asked, "Do you think your mother has been loving toward you in all of this?"

Helen looked stunned. "Of course!"

"Do you show love that way, Helen?"

"No...but I know my mother loves me no matter what I do."

"How?"

"Well...I guess I...I've just assumed that she loves me."

I could tell that Helen was offended by my questions about her mother's love for her. We finished lunch with some small talk and then graciously parted.

A few days later, Helen phoned me. She wanted to talk again, so I met her and Ken for coffee.

Helen began, "Maybe you were right. Maybe...but I hurt so bad, I feel so guilty all the time...but I just know she loves me." Helen began to cry. Ken put his arm around her.

I asked her, "Have you ever felt angry with your mother when she is being critical of you?"

"No...no, I haven't."

"Why not?" I asked, "Wouldn't anger be a normal response to someone who has condemned you, to someone who has hurt you?"

"Well...I guess so."

"Helen, how would you want your mother to treat you?"

Her eyes brightened. (She had obviously dreamed of this many times.) "She would affirm me, love me even if I'm overweight, talk *to* me—not *at* me, listen to me. We'd be friends. We'd do fun things together." She paused then and said, "She wouldn't slam the door of my room and leave me crying all alone."

Helen raised her voice, "But she never did those thoughtful and kind things! Never! She always made me wear the clothes she picked out for me. Even in high school."

Then Helen broke into uncontrollable weeping. Ken asked her gently, "What is it, honey?"

Helen looked up through her tears and sobbed, "She even made me take back a gown I'd bought for a big party. She made me wear one that she picked out. It was horrible! Everybody laughed at me!" Her voice calmed. "I haven't thought of that in years."

During several subsequent conversations, Helen started getting in touch with her deep hurt and repressed anger. It was the beginning of objectivity. It was the beginning of healing.

Helen was wearing the glasses of codependency. These glasses distorted reality and caused her to interpret life incorrectly. She thought that she was responsible for making her mother happy. When she failed, she felt guilty.

~

Why are codependents unable to see reality clearly? Why do they lack objectivity? There are basically two reasons. First, they have an impaired ability to compare reality with unreality. If the environment of their families has been steeped in deception and denial, then they, too, will probably be deceived and lack objectivity. Codependent children believe their parents are god-like. They conclude that however their parents treat them is how life really is. If their parents are loving, they surmise that they are lovable. If, however, the parents are manipulative, condemning, or neglectful, the children usually conclude that it is somehow their own fault, not their parents'. They see themselves as unlovable and unworthy of love and attention, all the while believing that their parents are always good and right. It is a convoluted, distorted, and tragic perspective. Similarly, marrying or establishing any strong relationship with a person who has a compulsive disorder can slowly erode a person's objectivity. The dysfunctional person lives a lie and expects everyone around him to live it, too!

The second reason codependents lack objectivity is that they fear reality. Solving other people's crises takes so much of the codependent's energy that the prospect of any additional pain or anger is simply too much to bear. Glimpses of reality are so painful that he is afraid of being overwhelmed by it in his own life. This perception is at least partially true. Objectivity does often bring great pain and anger. At times, it can seem truly overwhelming. But reality, with all its hurt and anger, is absolutely necessary before healing can occur. Crawling inside an emotional turtle shell may provide temporary relief from the harshness of reality, but it ultimately brings more long-term pain and prevents the process of healing.

A part of this fear of reality is the fear of losing one's identity. However broken and painful a codependent's self-concept may be, it is all that he has! The fear of losing that morsel of identity is very threatening. Strangely, he chooses to cling to a dysfunctional person who brings him pain, abuse, and neglect, instead of turning to reality, undergoing a healing process, and experiencing love, freedom, and strength. The term *denial* (lack of objectivity) may sound fairly benign, but it is powerful and insidious. Such a lack of objectivity can take many forms. Some people have learned to be very perceptive about others but not at all perceptive about themselves. Others have lost perception on most everything.

Some rescuers may well say, "I must not have this problem because my friends say I'm very perceptive." That may be true. One friend of mine can pick up the "vibes" of other people incredibly well and almost read their minds, but he has a very difficult time seeing the effects of his own painful past. For people like him, perception is a defense mechanism. In order to please others, gain approval, and survive the abrasive environment, such people learn to perceive exactly what they need to say and do. Although they are able to "read" others very well, they can't see that they have lost their own identity and have become virtual puppets, dancing on the strings of those whom they want to please (or whose condemnation they want to avoid).

A codependent who is perceptive about others, but not about himself, is like a man looking through the periscope of a submarine. He can clearly see the waves, the sky, and the ships around him, but he can't see himself or what's going on in the sub. He may be hit by depth charges from destroyers, but he can't see the damage because he's still looking through the periscope. (And a submarine, like codependency, is designed to take you down!)

Other codependents have a completely opposite defense mechanism. Instead of developing a finely tuned sense of perception so they can read people and win approval, they erect an emotional wall around themselves to block out their pain. They exist in a kind of emotional racquetball court, surrounded by walls and unable to realize how their actions and words are perceived by others. Erecting these walls may block some of the painful emotions of hurt and rejection, but the walls also prevent people from experiencing many pleasant emotions like love, warmth, intimacy, and joy. Walls are not selective about the emotions they block.

Codependents tend to see life in black or white, seldom in shades of gray. People and circumstances are perceived as being either wonderful or awful. One friend described a coworker to me a few months ago: "He's doing a fantastic job! He is really mature and a hard worker. I'm so glad to be working with him!" But later, the coworker had fallen from grace. My friend excoriated him: "I can't believe what a jerk he is! He has screwed up everything he's touched!" I wondered how this could be the same person he told me about a couple of months ago.

A codependent often exaggerates. Making people or situations seem a little *worse* than they really are (black) gives him a sense of identity, of importance. It causes others to become more concerned for him than they might be if he were more objective. Similarly, making people or situations seem a little *better* than they really are (white) makes him look better and more impressive. This is the codependent's goal in relationships: to impress people and/or to get them to feel sorry for him.

Other numerous factors, perceptions, and defense mechanisms prevent the codependent from seeing the truth. Several are listed below.

Selective Filtering of Information—The codependent's mental "grid" filters out a substantial amount of truth. She hears and sees only what she dreads. For example, when her bulimic sister says, for the umpteenth time, "It's over. I'm never going to binge and purge again," the codependent wants to believe it so badly that she feels great relief and joy—even though her sister's record of keeping promises is abysmal. Or, if a codependent is given a performance review at work with twenty things marked "Excellent" and one "Needs Improvement," he will be heartbroken. His mind will be consumed by the one area that needs some improvement instead of the report of his great work in the vast majority of his job.

Defending the Offender—Instead of honestly feeling the hurt of betrayal and experiencing the anger of being abused or neglected, the codependent will usually defend the offender. *It's not really her fault,* she surmises. *She couldn't help it, and besides, it doesn't bother me when she curses me like that. I'm used to it by now.* Or, *Yes, it hurts when he treats me that way, but I feel so sorry for him. He wants to stop drinking, but he just can't.*

Redefining the Pain—Being objective about their deep hurt and seething anger may be painful and/or guilt-inducing for codependents. But even worse is repressing these emotions which often causes psychosomatic illnesses. Many people who experience the tremendous stress of pain, anger, and guilt develop severe tension headaches, but instead of admitting to their stress, they say that they are having "migraine headaches." One man told me about his "migraines." His description was not of a one-sided, light-sensitive, throbbing pain at all. It was tension, but calling it a migraine redefined the pain to make it less threatening. A tension headache means he has stress to deal with. But a migraine is a vascular problem—no culpability there! A host of other labels are given to ailments that shift the source of the problem from repressed emotions to a purely physical cause. (This, of course, does not mean that every sickness experienced by a codependent is caused entirely by repressed emotions. Buried emotions do, however, lower our resistance to all kinds of physical problems.)

Pronouncements of Perception—A codependent will often announce an acute understanding of life's situations, even though he may not have a clear perception at all. It's as if his proclamations somehow make his perceptions accurate. He may say, "Oh yes, I see it all now!" Or she may proclaim, "I don't need his love and acceptance. It has never bothered me that he doesn't care about me." These kinds of statements are both the result of poor perception and the means for further denial in the future. If a person feels like his perception is accurate when it's not, then that inaccuracy acts as a defense mechanism which prevents him from seeing reality and feeling pain.

Peer Pressure—The intense peer pressure that adolescents face is difficult for even the most stable teenager to cope with because of the normal adolescent desire to be accepted. The added pressure felt by a codependent teenager is indeed intense. Dealing with both peer pressure and objective reality is a double whammy! And it is almost as difficult for young adults who experience the peer pressure of entering the "real world" after high school or college.

Too often, objectivity doesn't come until a codependent is in his thirties, forties, or fifties. The formative, wonderful years of youth have been wasted in the oppressive combination of peer pressure, denial, rescuing, guilt, and pain.

Diversions—I've heard it said that "activities are often the anesthetic to deaden the pain of an empty life." All kinds of activities are used by codependents to keep themselves so busy that they don't have time to reflect or feel. Working seventy to eighty hours a week, participating in clubs or sports, watching television and many other diversions keep them preoccupied. Most codependents are unaware that the reason their lives seem empty is because they have suppressed emotional pain. They may have a vague sense that something is wrong, but they have no idea what it is. Most reject any suggestion that they are trying to deal with repressed emotions through endless activities.

Exchanged Emotions—Because codependents haven't experienced very much true love, intimacy, genuine support, or encouragement, they often substitute one emotion for another. For instance, one woman (the wife of an alcoholic) equated worry with love. She always seemed to be worrying about her son, but she very seldom expressed genuine affection for him. She had substituted the intensity of her worry for the love that he actually needed. Others may use condemnation and praise to manipulate rather than simply loving. Some may substitute anger with a stoic calm that has the appearance of peacefulness, but which, in reality, is denial.

Euphemisms—To avoid dealing with objectivity about their emotions, codependents often use words that don't accurately reflect how they really feel. The classic example of this is the use of *frustrated* instead of *angry*. People seem to think that it's OK to be frustrated with someone, but real anger is a different story. Anger is too threatening for the codependent to admit, so he alters his words to make his emotions seem less severe. Though the word *frustrated* is perfectly legitimate to describe a mildly negative emotion, it is much overused. In our office, we have agreed not to use the word *frustrated*, and to go ahead and say that we are angry. Our staff found this to be difficult at first, but after a few days the honesty was very refreshing!

A Warped Sense of Responsibility

The second primary characteristic of codependency is a warped sense of responsibility. As we have seen, a codependent often feels unloved. He usually feels that he doesn't have worth or value. How, then, can he gain the value, love, and respect he so desperately wants? He tries to do this by helping others. When he or she helps somebody, it produces a temporary high: *I'm somebody. I'm appreciated. I have value.* The other person, especially when dysfunctional, cooperates nicely. He is glad for the codependent to solve his problems and rescue him. A treadmill develops of endless problems and a desperate problem-solver; of a needy person and a rescuer.

For the codependent, taking care of others becomes a consuming lifestyle. In his role as caretaker, he is like the man looking through the periscope of the submarine. He doesn't see the need to have his own identity, his own dreams, his own emotions, and his own schedule. He is driven to be and do and feel what other people want him to be and do and feel. He believes that doing anything for himself is "selfish."

It has been said that a codependent person can't say no, but that isn't true. He *can* say no, though when he does, he feels terribly guilty for "being so selfish."

The codependent—the rescuer—lacks objectivity about what the dependent person really needs. The other person doesn't always need to be rescued! He may need to be left alone, or to learn to be responsible for himself.

Dysfunctional people need to discover how to solve their own problems. They don't need to be rescued all the time. Rescuing only perpetuates their problems instead of solving them.

The codependent becomes a rescuer in an attempt to meet his craving for identity. He needs to be needed, so he inadvertently make problems worse by looking for every need he can meet. In the process, he makes little needs into big ones so he will feel more significant. He reads every facial expression and tone of voice so he can say or do just the right thing to make someone else happy. Then, when he has rescued the other person, he feels great—for a while. And if he fails, he feels miserable because the very basis of his self-worth has been shaken.

The emotions of a codependent are dependent on the responses of other people. For instance:

- *If the needy person is angry, it must be my fault. I feel guilty.*
- *If she is sad, I must have done something to hurt her feelings.*
- *If she is afraid, I need to comfort and protect her.*
- *If he is happy, I must have helped him!*

The dependent relationship also works in the other direction:

- *If I am angry, he needs to change how he treats me.*
- *If I am sad, it's her fault.*
- *If I am afraid, he needs to protect me.*
- *If I am happy, it is because she appreciates me.*

In addition to assuming the responsibility of making others happy, codependents expect those people to make them happy. Personal responsibility, where each person is responsible for himself is seldom considered! When a child in a dysfunctional family takes responsibility for his parents' happiness, he effectually becomes a parent to his parents. They should be nurturing, protecting, and providing for him, yet he takes the responsibility of nurturing, protecting, and providing for them. Roles are reversed: the parents are needy and the child is forced to assume adult responsibilities. He isn't allowed to go through a normal, healthy process of developing his self-concept and identity. He learns to deny his childish emotions and thus stops his development. The resulting damage is deep and prolonged. Children who have "parented" their parents often expect to be parented by their own children.

The Savior Complex/The Judas Complex

Linda explained to me that she feels responsible for her parents, her husband, her friends, her job, and everything else with which she comes into contact. She said, "I feel like I need to solve everybody's problems. Nobody else will do it if I don't."

A striking parallel hit me, "You feel like a savior, don't you?" I asked.

Her eyes lit up, then she smiled. "Yes, I do. I guess I'm taking somebody else's role." She laughed at her insight.

A codependent feels like he is either a savior or a Judas, one who rescues or one who betrays, one who helps or one who fails to help. These black-or-white perceptions of himself often change in a heartbeat, depending on whether the other person is happy or angry with him.

A codependent in his savior mode may believe that he can do no wrong in his quest to rescue everyone who is in need. His creed is:

- *If someone has a need, I'll meet it!*
- *If there's not a need, I'll find one and then meet it!*
- *If there's a small need, I'll make it a large one. Then I'll feel even better when I meet it!*

- *Even if nobody wants help, I'll help anyway!*
- *After I've helped, I'll feel good about myself!* (His family says, "We knew we could count on you.")

A person with a savior complex thinks he is indispensable. He believes that whatever *he* is doing is absolutely the most important thing in the world! Nobody else's role even comes close.

But in the Judas mode, the outlook is quite different. The mood is one of failure and despair. One man explained, "I feel like I have to rescue people, but I'm so afraid of failing that I'm paralyzed." He lives with tremendous tension and heartache. Paralyzing fear and withdrawal prevent the person with a Judas complex from actively rescuing.

This withdrawal may be an occasional response for most codependents, but the Judas complex is most common for the "lost child" and the "scapegoat." Neither the lost child nor the scapegoat may see himself as a codependent, though both are. Both want (or at some point, wanted) to rescue others just like a codependent in the savior mode (an *enabler*, a *hero*, or a *mascot*), but they can't. The creed of these people is:

- *People need me, but I can't help them.*
- *Others' needs are enormous, and I feel awful that I can't help.*
- *Every time I try to help, I mess up.*
- *No matter what I do, it's wrong.*
- *If I try, I fail. If I don't try, I fail. I am a miserable failure.* (He believes his family would say, "We thought we could count on you, but I guess we can't.")

It is not at all unusual for a person with a savior complex to nosedive into a Judas complex. There are three basic ways this can happen: (1) He tries to help, but he fails. (2) He tries to help, but he isn't appreciated. (3) He doesn't even try because he's sure he will fail. In any of these situations, his response is usually withdrawal, guilt, loneliness, anger, self-condemnation, and hopelessness.

The charts that follow illustrate the savior and Judas complexes and correspond roughly to the aforementioned black-and-white extremes the codependent demonstrates due to his lack of objectivity. The difference is that these charts describe the codependent's extremes in his self-concept, either as a rescuer or a betrayer.

A person who is either very skilled at pleasing people (or who is very young and hasn't experienced enough crushing blows of failure) may be in a chronic savior pattern. Often, someone in this condition sees himself as a very healthy and successful person, not as the person he really is. Only a few times has he ever felt like a Judas.

Chronic Savior Pattern

Savior
(I can help you.)

Judas
(I'll let you down.)

A person who has experienced more criticism gradually loses confidence in himself. His chart may look like this:

Mixed Savior/Judas Pattern

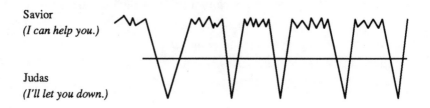

Savior
(I can help you.)

Judas
(I'll let you down.)

Through any number of painful circumstances and manipulative, condemning people, a person's self-concept may erode to a point where it is characterized almost completely by guilt, despair, anger, loneliness, and hopelessness. This may happen when he is a child, or much later. His life will then be characterized by a chronic Judas pattern:

Chronic Judas Pattern

Savior
(I can help you.)

Judas
(I'll let you down.)

The savior and Judas complexes are flip sides of the same coin. Both stem from the need for a sense of worth and to be loved and accepted. The savior feels he is accomplishing that goal. The Judas fears he can't.

The codependent person puts himself in a no-win situation. Whether he successfully rescues someone or fails to rescue, his involvement results in the personal and relational maladies described below.

Codependents neglect themselves. By focusing on others' needs, codependents fail to see their own needs. They need their own identity, their own opinions, their own time, their own friends, and their own feelings.

Codependents resent being saviors. Codependents rescue others to feel good about themselves, but this good feeling often dissipates rather quickly. They rescue, then they get angry that someone has taken advantage of them, then they feel sorry for themselves. This cycle of rescue/anger/self-pity (or a three-person triangle of rescuer/persecutor/victim) is the insight of Stephen B. Karpman and is called the Karpman Drama Triangle.[1]

Codependents threaten, but continue rescuing. When he feels anger and self-pity, a codependent will threaten to stop helping someone, especially another codependent or a person with a compulsive disorder. He says, "That's the limit! That's as far as I go! You have to change your behavior!" But when these threats are consistently followed by more fixing, solving, and rescuing, they become meaningless. The one threatened learns he can continue to do as he pleases. He knows he will always be rescued.

Codependents lack objectivity about serving and helping others. Because so much of their lives is spent in helping others, codependents often see themselves as humble (or abused) servants. Yet there is a great difference between helping people because you *want* to, and feeling that you *have* to help others to prevent a loss of value and worth. The former is loving service; the latter is codependency.

Codependents take themselves too seriously. Several years ago, a coworker told me that I was taking myself too seriously and that I should lighten up. My initial response was to think, *Fine! I'll just give up trying to have a sense of self-worth by accomplishing enough to win the respect and approval of other people.* My friend was right, of course. I *was* much too serious (and probably still am), but telling me not to take myself seriously didn't solve the problem. A person's self-worth and value is serious, but codependent behavior is not the solution. It is part of the problem.

Controlled/Controlling

Without the secure moorings of love, acceptance, and significance, the codependent feels responsible for everything, but confident in nothing. He tries to find his security by pleasing people, by being right, and by doing right things in the correct way. He feels something like a puppet, dancing on the strings of praise and condemnation, easily controlled by the desires of others. Paradoxically, he wants to be in absolute control of his own life so he won't fail. He also wants to control the behavior of others so that they will add to, and not subtract from, his ability to perform well and please people.

Controlled by Others—Like everyone else, codependents need love and respect, but having been deprived of these precious commodities, they determine to do whatever it takes to win the approval and value they crave. Their means to that end is to make people happy. Their chief fear is that people will be unhappy with them. Those around them quickly learn which of the codependent's buttons to push. Skillful use of praise and condemnation artfully manipulates the codependent.

The codependent is pressured to do more and to be more for the other person. He hears statements like:

- "A score of 95 on an exam isn't good enough."
- "I wish you'd get that promotion. I'd be so proud of you!"
- "Why do you drive that piece of junk?"
- "I'm proud of you for doing so well. I can't wait to tell my friends!"
- "You are so wonderful to help me. I wish your sister was as kind as you are."
- "You wouldn't be stupid enough to vote for somebody like that, would you?"
- "I wish you had come. I really needed you."
- "My goodness, what an unusual hair style. I'm sure it will look better when it grows out."

The one who is controlling you probably believes he is doing you a great favor. He justifies his control over you with statements such as:

- "I'm only saying this for your own good...because I love you."
- "I know what's best for you. In fact, I know you better than you know yourself."
- "I'm your father. If I can't say this to you, who can?"
- "If it weren't for me, there's no telling what a mess you'd make of your life!"

These and a myriad of other statements range from delicate to severe manipulation. Each one may innocently sound like a harmless question or observation. But in the context of codependency where a person feels worthless and desperate for love and affirmation, such statements constitute an attack designed to change behavior through praise or condemnation. And it works!

Guilt is a primary motivator which usually results in a "have to" mentality. The perceived risks of losing love and/or respect are too great to allow failure. Consequently, the codependent is driven. He is obsessive-compulsive. He has to do the right thing, make the clever remark, wear the right clothes, look the right way and, in short, be perfect. (That's not asking too much, is it?) In addition to being driven, he is usually very compliant. He will do anything for anybody at any time with a smile—at least for a while.

Another motivating factor is comparison. The codependent is compared to other members of the family, coworkers, relatives, and anybody else who might urge him to do more. A friend told me of her experience with such tactics. Every month or so her mother tells her: "My friends' children are always doing nice things for them. They buy them clothes, take them on vacations, and buy them jewelry and nice furniture. Their children are there whenever they are needed." Then she adds the clincher: "I guess I'll just have to take care of myself." Is this a neutral statement of fact, a statement of independence? No way! This mother used comparison to attempt to manipulate her daughter! Manipulation is not benign. It is evil, seductive, and destructive.

Control of Self—Codependents define themselves by what they do, how they look, and how well they accomplish tasks. They have to be right. They have to be in control of their lives. The rest of their lives is so chaotic (with a dependent parent or spouse) that they have a strong need to control any possible area of their lives.

As is usually the case with codependents, there are two extremes: being obsessive-compulsive to gain control of life, or giving up and withdrawing. Some codependents must have order in their lives. Things are in boxes—neatly labeled, of course. The home is tidy, clothes are immaculate, makeup is worn perfectly, every hair is in place, the car is clean (with the tank filled), and work is done on time with excellence. Schedules are meticulously drawn up to aid maximum efficiency and minimize distractions. But at best, their sense of satisfaction for doing a job well is very short-lived. It has to be done again tomorrow, and next week, and next month, and....

Control of Others—How the codependent relates to others is usually a mirror of his relationship with the compulsive person in his life. He hates the way he has been treated, yet may treat others the same way. Modeling is a powerful teacher which shapes our patterns of behavior.

Fixers manipulate others by using the same techniques of praise and condemnation that have been used on them. They use their wit and humor to impress people. Codependents usually have excellent minds and develop strong communication skills to win acceptance. They use sarcasm to cut people to ribbons ("Just kidding!") along with praise, anger, and withdrawal to get people to do what they want them to do.

In the attempt to control people, rescuers usually fall into two extremes again. On the one hand, they may try to "mother" people (perhaps *smother* would be a better word), and they shape opinions and habits by constant attention through both praise and criticism. Rescuers don't let others out of their sight for long. Some go beyond mothering and become like dictators, barking orders and exercising their real or perceived authority in others' lives.

On the other end of the continuum is withdrawal. A person may become so tired of trying to control others, or may feel so inadequate and worthless, that he believes no one will do what he wants. His poor self-concept overcomes his desire to manipulate, and he gives up.

The paradox for the codependent is that while he is trying to control others, he is also being controlled *by* them. He wants them to perform and then appreciate his efforts to help, but he still gets his self-worth from their approval. One man tried to get his wife, who was addicted to prescription drugs, to pull her act together because her behavior might cost him a promotion. He pleaded and threatened in his attempt to control her behavior, but instead, she controlled him. She could be happy when she wanted, or angry or sad when she chose. That way, she could get him to do almost anything for her. The rabbit was chasing the dog.

Codependents desperately need to be loved. They desperately need to feel that they have a sense of worth. When these needs are unmet, some will try to avoid the pain by being indecisive and passive, while others will try to win approval by being right. Most are a blend of the two. Certain people or situations cause withdrawal while other times the codependent will take a stand, state opinions forcefully, and hope people like what he says. Both avenues are strategies toward the same goal: avoiding pain and winning approval.

Summary

A Lack of Objectivity

1. What are some ways by which you can tell if your friend or relative perceives life in the extremes of black and white? Name the words, attitudes, and actions he might use:

2. Does he tend to be more extreme (black or white) around certain people or in certain situations? If so, with whom and when?

3. Examine each of the "blinders" described previously in this chapter. To what degree do each of these block your friend's or relative's perception of reality, enabling him to avoid pain?

Selective filtering of information

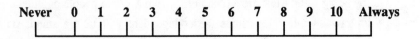

| Never | 0 | 1 | 2 | 3 | 4 | 5 | 6 | 7 | 8 | 9 | 10 | Always |

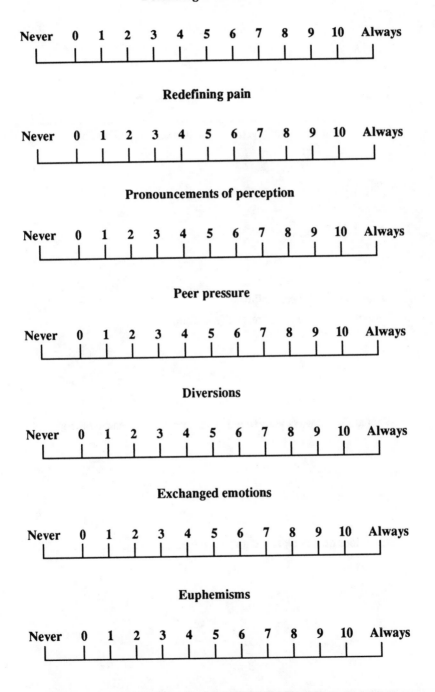

Defending the offender

Never   0   1   2   3   4   5   6   7   8   9   10   Always

Redefining pain

Never   0   1   2   3   4   5   6   7   8   9   10   Always

Pronouncements of perception

Never   0   1   2   3   4   5   6   7   8   9   10   Always

Peer pressure

Never   0   1   2   3   4   5   6   7   8   9   10   Always

Diversions

Never   0   1   2   3   4   5   6   7   8   9   10   Always

Exchanged emotions

Never   0   1   2   3   4   5   6   7   8   9   10   Always

Euphemisms

Never   0   1   2   3   4   5   6   7   8   9   10   Always

4. How would increased objectivity affect his life?

5. Name several ways and several people that can help him to be more objective. Be specific:

A Warped Sense of Responsibility

1. Define what it means to "rescue" someone:

2. What are some ways your friend or relative tries to rescue others?

3. When does he feel like a savior? How does he act?

4. When does he feel like a Judas? How does he act?

5. Can he say "no" without feeling guilty?

6. Identify and describe the results of a warped sense of responsibility in your friend or relative's life:

   a) How does he prevent others from developing responsibility? What are the results of these actions?

   b) How does he neglect himself? Name some results of this behavior:

   c) Is he a resentful savior? If so, how does this affect him, you and others?

d) Does he ever threaten to stop rescuing, only to continue doing so? Name some results of these actions:

e) Does he seem to lack objectivity about serving and helping others? Describe how this affects him and those he "helps" or "serves":

7. How would his life be different if he weren't compelled to help, fix, and rescue? How would his self-concept, his time, his values, and his relationships be affected?

Controlled/Controlling

1. Does your friend or relative give in to pressure easily? List some instances when he has been easily manipulated by criticism, fear, the desire for acceptance or position, etc.

2. How does he feel and act when he is manipulated and gives in?

3. How does he feel and act when he is manipulated and doesn't give in?

4. Does he try to control your schedule, your lifestyle, your emotions, etc.? If so, how? What are the results?

5. Describe some ways that people try to control others:

6. How did (does) your friend or relative's family try to control him? In what ways is this like or unlike how he tries to control others?

7. What are some situations in which he becomes passive and indecisive because he is afraid to fail?

8. In what situations does he feel that he has to be right and that people have to agree with him?

Endnotes

[1] Claude M. Steiner, *Scripts People Live* (New York: Grove Press, 1974), as quoted by Melody Beattie, *Codependent No More*, p. 77.

Chapter 4

The Corollary Characteristics of Codependency

Many people who are overly responsible, easily manipulated, and controlling people are struggling with problems from their bonding stage of development. The corollary characteristics of codependency describe some of these complicating and painful difficulties: hurt and anger, guilt and loneliness.

Hurt and Anger

Why do some people experience neglect or anger and get over it fairly easily, while codependents either react much more strongly or not at all?

You might expect active physical and/or verbal abuse in a dysfunctional family to leave the codependent feeling deeply hurt and angered by the ones who have hurt him. But the passive abuse of neglect and withdrawal are equally devastating.

The family that is supposed to provide warmth and worth provides pain instead. The codependent (at least the enabler, the hero, and the mascot) then may attempt to please and rescue the one(s) hurting him in order to win the love and approval he so desperately wants. Yet any temporary rewards for his attempts to rescue will not meet his need for unconditional love. His hurt and anger will continue to grow. He is trapped in a system which, by withholding love and affection, fuels his compulsion to rescue.

To a relatively stable person, offenses may feel like a fist hitting an arm. It hurts for a while, but the pain soon disappears. The same blow to a codependent is more severe. His emotional arm is already broken, so the pain of being hit is much more overbearing. And it lasts much longer.

Hurt and anger go hand-in-glove. Hurt is the result of not being loved or valued. It comes from feeling abandoned, used, and condemned. Anger is the reaction toward the source of the hurt.

These painful emotions are not only products of the codependent's past. They are a part of his reality every day. In trying to rescue the one who has hurt him, he gets hurt again and again. And sooner or later, he gets angry.

The pain and anger within a codependent's soul are deep and black. Even a glimpse of them can seem overwhelming, so he erects elaborate defense mechanisms to block pain and to control anger. These defensive "layers" include a denial of reality, the need to please people, being in control, keeping people at a distance, being numb to feelings, displacing anger, excusing the offender(s), and many other variations. Some use different defenses for different circumstances, but most develop several layers to ensure their protection.

Defense mechanisms bring short-term gain, but they yield long-term losses by preventing us from beginning the healing process. These layers of defense mechanisms need to be peeled away to expose pain and anger so these issues can be dealt with.

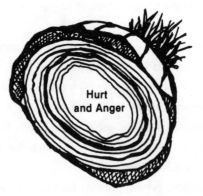

Objectivity is the first step toward healing. We will gain insight by examining some common ways that codependents respond to their hurt and anger.

Numbness—"I don't want to feel this way, so I won't." This is a personal philosophy for some people. The pain is too great, so the person blocks it out. Frightened by his anger, he acts like it's not there. The codependent is forced to live life at a surface level emotionally. He knows that what's underneath is simply too much to bear. Consequently, his emotions and relationships are superficial.

One young lady described her parents who divorced when she was seven. Her father remarried and moved away. Her mother went to work to support her and her brother. Her father sent her gifts for a couple of years after he left, but he later faded from her life. Her mother was frazzled and frantic as an abandoned, working, single parent.

"How do you think your parents' divorce has affected you?" I asked.

"Oh, not much at all."

"Do you miss your father?"

"No, not really."

"Do you feel especially close to your mother since she's taking care of you so well?"

"Yeah, I guess so...well, we're not *that* close."

She seemed a bit detached, so I asked a different question. "What makes you really happy? What do you really enjoy?"

She thought for a minute. "I can't think of anything."

"Then what makes you really angry? What upsets you?"

"Not much," she replied blankly. "I don't feel much of anything."

Over the next several months as we talked more about her past, she began to feel more. Some of her feelings were painful. Some were pleasant. It was a mixed bag, but she was becoming more in touch with her life and her feelings.

Sometimes codependents conclude that painful feelings must be wrong. They try to make others happy, yet suppress their own feelings. People can't be picky about which aspects of their emotions they suppress. They can't stifle bad feelings and only enjoy good ones. When they repress painful feelings, they quell the enjoyable ones, too.

Another way people may try to numb pain is by staying so busy that they don't have time to reflect. We can perpetuate a numb feeling. The theme song for such people is Carly Simon's, "Haven't Got Time for the Pain." Lives filled with activities and superficial relationships don't have time to feel pain.

Pain Without Gain—Some people may wish for numbness, yet feel intense emotional pain. They hurt so badly they can hardly stand it. They feel they are being hopelessly crushed. An intense feeling of loss with no hope of gain consumes them. They feel as though they've been broken into a million pieces, and there isn't any glue to fix them. They experience no healing—only hurt.

But they don't want to admit this kind of hurt to others, so they put up a facade of competence and happiness. Few people ever realize the blackness that lurks beneath the neon exterior of these people. Their belief that they are inherently bad people, unworthy of love, leads to self-condemnation and self-hatred. Some think and say terrible things about themselves. They call themselves horrible, degrading names that would be described as hatred and abuse if coming from someone else. But they don't consider it abuse because they believe that they deserve that kind of treatment.

Excusing the Offender/Blaming Ourselves—Often, where there is hurt without healing, there is no anger toward the offender. Anger is displaced, and the offender is excused. The desire to "believe the best" of the one causing the hurt blocks objectivity. Instead of blaming him, the codependent blames himself.

Displaced Anger—Sometimes a codependent's repressed anger is directed toward people or things that have nothing to do with its cause. Such anger surfaces at odd times and in unexpected ways. It may also be disproportionate in its intensity. Suppressed anger may explode like a tube of toothpaste that is squeezed until it pops and toothpaste squirts in all directions. Whoever happens to be around during the "explosion" is likely to receive a disproportionate amount of anger.

Using Self-Pity and Anger to Manipulate Others—Hurt and anger are powerful emotions. They affect people deeply and can be used to manipulate others to care about us and dance to our tune. The codependent is the product of such manipulation, but he quickly learns to use these powerful forces on others as well. Most become just as effective in eliciting the responses of pity and fear (poor counterfeits of love and respect that they really want and need).

Memories—When a person begins to get in touch with the pain of his past, he will often remember events that have long been buried in his mind and heart. The hurt and anger that these memories evoke are painful. Some people may interpret this pain as going backward, but it is actually progress.

A friend of mine recently remembered that he had been hospitalized for an ulcer when he was 10 years old. He had not remembered that event for 25 years, but instantly he could vividly recall minute details of his pain, his confusion, and specific conversations with doctors and nurses. These memories flooded his heart with pain as he relived the event. He was sad and depressed for several weeks, but as he processed the pain, he developed a new understanding of himself and a new sense of freedom from the bondage of the past.

At the core of a codependent's heart are hurt and anger—results of the abuse, manipulation, and/or neglect experienced in a dysfunctional relationship. He tries to obstruct the pain and control the anger any way he can, but his defense mechanisms are counterproductive. He needs objectivity that reveals truth. He needs patience to go through the process of pain so that healing can take place. But it's not time for solutions yet. He must also develop objectivity about guilt and loneliness.

Guilt

Codependents usually feel guilty, either for what they've done or what they haven't done. They feel guilty for what they've said, haven't said, felt, and haven't felt. They feel guilty for just about everything. Often such quantities of guilt produce feelings of worthlessness and shame.

Most codependents get their worth—their identity—from what they do for other people. Some of them rescue, help, and enable. But no matter how much they do for others, it's never enough. Others have given up on rescuing. They withdraw into the loneliness of isolation or rebel against the compulsion to help others. That's the trap of living in a dysfunctional family. They rescue, but they are ultimately rejected. If they fail to rescue, they are rejected. Lacking objectivity, he concludes: *It's my fault. If I were a better person, they would love me.* He's haunted by the shame that he hasn't measured up.

The guilt and shame I am referring to are not the kind that promote an objective judgment of our offense. If you have been caught going 85 m.p.h. on the highway and the judge pronounces, "Guilty as charged," that is objective guilt. In that sense, all mankind stands before God as guilty and in need of the forgiveness and acceptance of the cross.

But the guilt we are looking at in this chapter is a different kind. It is guilt without objectivity, devoid of forgiveness, with no real hope of love and acceptance. It is the painful, gnawing perception that you are worthless, unacceptable, and can never do enough to be loved, no matter how hard you try.

There is a vast difference between these two kinds of guilt. One produces an urgent sorrow that leads to positive, refreshing change. The other leads to a hopeless sorrow that only crushes. The apostle Paul described positive and negative guilt in his second letter to the Corinthian believers:

> *I now rejoice, not that you were made sorrowful, but that you were made sorrowful to the point of repentance; for you were made sorrowful according to the will of God, in order that you might not suffer loss in anything through us.*
>
> *For the sorrow that is according to the will of God produces a repentance without regret, leading to salvation; but the sorrow of the world produces death.*
>
> 2 Corinthians 7:9-10

The realization of personal wrong brings hope and change when coupled with a knowledge of forgiveness. But the realization of personal wrong without that forgiveness brings bitter pangs of condemnation and hopelessness. In dysfunctional families, personal wrongs are magnified while forgiveness, love, and acceptance are withheld. Those bitter pangs of condemnation are a way of life for the codependent.

Guilt Crushes—Guilt crushes a person's dreams, desires, and personality. If his worth comes only from helping others, then he can't say no to anything or anyone. If he does say no, or even if he says yes and fails (or if he succeeds but others don't appreciate him), then his worth is shattered. Even success and praise bring only short-term relief in light of the nagging fear of losing approval.

All of us have done things that are wrong, but a codependent attaches greater weight to such wrongs than he does to forgiveness. He is deeply ashamed, feeling that at least some of those terrible things he has done cannot possibly be forgiven.

Rescuing is seen as life's greatest good by the codependent. Selfishness is the worst sin. After all, his very identity comes from being unselfish and giving until it hurts (and usually far beyond where it hurts)! When accused of selfishness, he feels a severe condemnation that threatens his only foundation: his ability to help others. This fact is clear to his dysfunctional family. The quickest way to get a codependent person to cower and give in is to pull out the big gun: "You're so selfish! How can you even think of not doing what I ask you to do?" This confirms his worthlessness and "pulls his strings."

Many of us from neglectful or abusive homes develop a deep sense of worthlessness. That worthlessness (or shame) can become self-hatred if we continue to turn our anger inward and despise ourselves. *Self-hatred* is an offensive term to many of us, but if we called other people the names we call ourselves, and if we thought of other people the way we think of ourselves, we would say we hate those other people. Our loathing of ourselves is genuine hatred for who we are, for what we're doing, and for what we believe we'll always be.

Self-hatred greatly complicates our needs and desires. Our self-hatred has developed because our deepest needs for love and security haven't been met. We hate the fact that we want and need so much, so we repress our desires, and the desires continue to grow without being fulfilled.

A friend of mine explained that he wants to be loved so badly that he has spent his entire life trying to please people in order to win their love. Though he tries so hard, his efforts only increase his sense of emptiness. Then he hates his desire because it only produces more pain. That hatred, in turn, drives him farther from people because he doesn't feel worthy to be loved by anyone. His emotions and thoughts are confused, complicated, and tragic.

Guilt Motivates—The guilt-ridden codependent surmises that the only way to win at life is to earn the respect of others. The hope of gaining acceptance and the threat of losing it are powerful motivators. They prompt the codependent to rescue people who take advantage of him and help people who don't appreciate him. Oh, he gets a little of the appreciation he craves. He gets just enough to keep him on the hook, but not enough to really satisfy him. So he keeps running on the endless treadmill of hope, guilt, and fear.

Motivation by guilt is usually associated with the desire to avoid condemnation or measure up to standards set by someone else. The codependent performs with a sense of urgency and desperation because he thinks he has to, not because he wants to. His motivation is characterized by *I have to* and *I can't* statements:

- *I have to accomplish this task today.*
- *I have to go here.*
- *I have to help this person in this way at this time.*
- *I have to say yes.*
- *I have to control my anger and hurt.*
- *I can't fail in this assignment.*
- *I can't let her down.*
- *I can't let my anger get out of control.*
- *I can't say no.*

Statements like these are the creed of the obsessive-compulsive codependent and are painful taunts of dismal failure to the one who has given up and withdrawn into passivity. Either way, they form the warp and woof of the codependent's mental fabric. His driving goal to acquire worth prevents his ability to say no, make his own decisions, relax, or enjoy.

Codependents live by *should's* and *ought's*—not by the confidence of security and significance. They are driven to have more, be more, say more, and do more. The carrot of self-worth dangles from the stick, always just out of reach. No matter how much he does, the codependent almost always has the nagging thought that *I should have done more.*

Using Guilt on Others—The law of sowing and reaping takes effect in the area of guilt just as it does in every other part of life. If guilt has been used to motivate and manipulate you, you will probably use it to manipulate others. It is a strange fact that even if you detest the way you have been treated, that model you have known is so strong that you may find yourself treating others the same way.

A father realized that he both condemned his children and withdrew his affection from them to manipulate their obedience. He felt terrible about it. He loathed and despised himself when he did it, but it was how his parents had treated him. It was the only way he knew to behave, even though he realized it was wrong and knew how much it had hurt him.

If you know a codependent, expect him to use the same words of praise and condemnation, actions, tone of voice, expressions, aggressive and angry behavior, withdrawal, or passivity that have been used to manipulate him. And understand that guilt is a way of life for the codependent. The nagging pain of believing, *There's something wrong with me, and I've got to fix it,* is a powerful and destructive force. We need to see this force for what it is: evil and destructive.

Loneliness

From the outside, codependents may appear to be the most social people in the world as they spend their lives giving, helping, and serving others. But inside they are lonely. Though they may occasionally capture a glimpse of love and respect, it usually fades all too quickly. Then, thinking they have been abandoned by both people and God, they feel empty and companionless. They distrust authority, believing that anyone above them is against them, and they build elaborate facades to hide their painful feelings of loneliness.

Abandoned by People—Sarah described her relationship with her cold, rigid, demanding husband. She longed for intimacy and affection, but what she got was a perfunctory physical relationship, enough money for groceries, and shallow conversation. In return, he expected her to keep the house spotless, cook like a French chef, and drop whatever she was doing whenever he wanted something. Her conclusion, like most codependents, was that the problem was her fault. "I guess I'm just not a good person," she said weakly, looking down at the floor. "I guess I'm not worthy of being loved." She began to cry.

Abusive or addicted (dependent) people usually give little and take a lot. In contrast, the codependent is like a tank of water with a slow drip coming in and a stream going out. The tank will flow for a while, but eventually it will run dry. The trickle can never fill the tank as long as the hole remains in the bottom. The codependent may get occasional encouragement, but he gives so much more time and emotional energy that he is perpetually "running on empty."

As the codependent gives and gives, a destructive sense of entitlement grows within him. He feels entitled to the appreciation and respect of others. Getting strokes becomes a compulsion. When he gets recognition of his efforts, he is satisfied like an alcoholic taking a drink. When he doesn't, he feels angry and abandoned, but he can't say anything or he might experience even more loneliness. He feels hopelessly trapped. He is unwilling to say how he feels— that he is hurt and angry—because he is afraid that people will withdraw from him. And if they go away, he'll be even more lonely.

Although he is desperate for intimacy, he doesn't feel lovable and is afraid of losing what little warmth he already has. The combination of these factors paralyzes and confuses him. One young lady who described her loneliness, desires, and fears seemed like a little girl who was crying, "I need help! Leave me alone!"

Abandoned by God—God's offer of unconditional love, forgiveness, and acceptance is available for codependents, of course, yet most feel distant from Him. They feel that He, too, disapproves of them, and that they can't do enough to please Him no matter how hard they try. It's no wonder they feel hopeless, hurt, and lonely. God is seen as their last hope. If *He* doesn't love them, who will?

The codependent's view of God is almost always the same as his view of his parents. If his parents neglected him, he will feel that God doesn't care. If his parents condemned him, he will think that God is harsh and demanding. Consequently, God is seen as part of the problem, not the solution.

Abandoned by Authority—Codependents tend to view authority figures the same way they view the addicted or abusive people in their lives—especially if those people are parents. They are often intensely loyal to bosses, pastors, or other kinds of leaders, and sometimes believe that the one in authority can do no wrong. They make others omnipotent because they feel so inadequate themselves. They will put up with all kinds of mistakes until, at last, the pendulum swings and suddenly the authority figure who could do no wrong suddenly can do nothing right.

The codependent wants to be accepted and appreciated by those who are in positions of importance and respect. He values their opinions of him highly, in fact, too highly. But he also has an innate sense that those in authority are out to get him, to use him, and to manipulate him. Depending on which end of these extremes the pendulum has swung (in his black-or-white perception), he sees the authority figure as either completely for or completely against him.

Introspection—A codependent tries to stifle pain by either putting up a wall and refusing to think about life, or by thinking about himself all day, every day. In this introspective mode, he analyzes his every word, conversation, action, and thought.

This seems paradoxical: he devotes his life to rescuing and helping others, yet thinks about himself all the time. But remember that his reasons for rescuing and helping are to gain a sense of worth, to be loved, and to earn the respect and appreciation that he so desperately wants.

There is a great difference between reflection and morbid introspection. Reflection is based on reality. It is objective, healthy, and not predisposed to condemnation. Morbid introspection is quite different. An introspective person digs through his thoughts, motives, and actions with twin hopes: to find and change the wrong in his life, and to find the right in his life so he can feel good about himself. Such incessant digging is not objective. It begins and continues with the person's underlying pessimistic assumption that, *There's something very wrong with me, and I've got to make it right.* Self-condemnation dominates his thinking. But feeling hurt and anger are not permitted (since they are considered "wrong"), so these painful feelings are internalized and the downward spiral continues.

Comparison—One of the prime by-products of introspection is comparison. A person who lacks security and significance needs some means of determining where he stands. Comparison is the perfect solution! He compares himself to others in terms of career advancements, wittiness, physical looks, and more.

The codependent is never at a loss of standards to use as comparisons because his dysfunctional relatives will usually help him. They will compare his clothes, his hair, his job, his children, his intellect, his athletic ability...as if he needs any help!

This tendency toward comparison feeds the fantasies of the introspective codependent. He imagines himself getting accolades and promotions, having beautiful things and accomplishing great feats of daring...all just a little bigger and better than someone else.

Facades—People often develop facades in childhood as a survival technique. Looking calm, cheerful, or tough enables them to shield their feelings. But as adults, these facades are detrimental because they prevent the development of honest and genuine relationships.

Codependents desperately want to be understood and to feel close to others, but they're afraid of rejection. Then they would hurt even more. To avoid this risk of additional pain, they protect themselves by appearing to be happy and well adjusted even when they are dying inside. They erect facades.

They don't say what they mean, and they don't mean what they say. To put it bluntly, they lie a lot. They say yes when they want to say no. They say they are just fine when they are feeling just a step or two away from suicide. They say they want to go somewhere because they think going there will make someone else happy enough to like them, when in fact, they don't want to go there at all. They get so wrapped up in making other people happy that they get numb and confused, and don't even know what they want!

They offer to help with a friendly smile even when they're so angry with that person they could spit nails. If their countenance slips and someone asks, "Is anything wrong?" they give an excuse that is usually partially true, but keeps others at arms-length: "Oh, I have a headache today," or "Yeah, I'm just not having a good day, but I'm all right."

They become masterful at selling themselves. They are enthusiastic about jobs, families, new hairstyles, and clothes. They find something good and milk it for all it's worth so that people will believe they are really doing well. But in reflective moments, they realize that what they've said is a lie—a facade—but they can't let others know the truth! As a result, they often feel dirty, guilty, and alone. Facades may protect codependents from the risks of intimacy, but they leave them lonely. When someone locks others out, he locks himself in.

The Codependent Christian

The Gospel of Jesus Christ is a message of freedom, forgiveness, hope, love, joy, and strength. It is the Good News, the most liberating and energizing power mankind has ever heard, or will ever hear! Yet through the distorted glasses of codependency, this phenomenal message is often perceived as oppressive, condemning, and guilt-inducing. Freedom is turned to bondage, forgiveness to guilt, hope to despair, love to condemnation, joy to pessimism, and divine strength to self-sufficiency.

But why is it so difficult for the codependent Christian to understand and apply God's grace? As in every other area of their lives, codependent Christians lack objectivity and balance, and react as extremists in regard to their spiritual commitment. Their desire for intimacy with God is either squelched by a view that God is cool, distant, and harsh, or the love of God is craved to such an extreme depth that they become "hypermystical" and feelings-oriented.

As we have seen, codependents have a warped sense of responsibility. Since they perceive their worth comes from their ability to perform, they are driven either to achieve as much as possible or to withdraw in hopelessness. But self-achievement is the exact opposite of humbly receiving the grace of God. So how does a person measure his performance so he can see if he has achieved value and worth? By doing what he knows he *should* do.

He divides life into distinct categories: the *have-to's* and the *can'ts*. This black-or-white set of options steals the fun and spontaneity from life. It also leaves a person with an overactive conscience—pride if he does well, despair if he doesn't, and a fear of failure and rejection no matter what.

The codependent who is a Christian adds the ought's and should's of Christianity to his already oppressive load of society's expectations. His wrong perspective of Christ and the Christian life oppresses him even further rather than providing much-needed peace. Instead of grace, he experiences guilt. It is grace that ultimately produces a *want-to* motivation, though it may take a long time to develop.

Many commands in Scripture are misinterpreted by codependent Christians and applied in the savior mode to gain a sense of worth. Some of these include:

- going the second mile to help someone
- turning the other cheek when someone hurts him
- loving those who don't love him
- giving cheerfully
- denying his own desires for the sake of others
- loving his neighbor as he loves himself
- having a disciplined life of prayer and Bible study
- letting no unwholesome word proceed from his mouth
- forgiving, loving, and accepting others as Christ does

The codependent Christian believes that he is expected to perform these commands (and all the others) perfectly, with feelings of love, peace, and joy at all times. In a good Christian life, he surmises, there is absolutely no room for hurt and anger.

His plight is further complicated by this denial of emotions. His hurt and anger are stuffed away with reasoning like: *A good Christian shouldn't feel this way...so I won't. It's so wonderful to be a Christian . . . (but I'm dying inside).*

Sooner or later, despair will catch up with him, and his thoughts will become something like:

- *If I were walking with God, I wouldn't have these problems.*
- *God has deserted me.*
- *Nobody cares about me. I'm all alone.*
- *Maybe I'm not really a Christian after all. Surely nobody who feels this way can be a Christian.*

When I first began to study codependency and saw it is such a problem, I wondered why the Scriptures didn't say anything about it. Then I realized, they do! Changing warped, codependent perceptions relates directly to the dominant themes of the Bible: the character of God, the doctrine of grace, the availability of unconditional love and acceptance not based on performance, God's declaration of our worth and value because of our identity in Christ, helping people for right reasons, and so forth. These transforming truths are not communicated in the language of 20th century psychology, but rather in that of the ancient writers. Still, they speak powerfully to the root needs of codependents: the needs for love, acceptance, worth, and value.

Superficial Solutions—Codependents want quick, simple solutions to fix themselves and other people. There's only one problem with easy answers— they don't work! Codependency is a deep, long-term problem. If the codependent's problem were primarily one of wrong action, it could be corrected relatively easily. But theirs is a problem of *perception*.

Instead of helping codependents overcome their warped perspectives, both society and the Christian culture usually *reinforce* codependency by valuing codependent behavior. Helping, fixing, enabling, intensity, motivation (manipulation), effectiveness, conscientiousness, and pleasing others are all considered virtues! Codependents often make the best employees and church workers because of the very characteristics that cause them such problems. In some Christian circles, the obsessive-compulsive drive of codependency is equated with a deep commitment to Christ! These two may seem similar on the outside. The activities, words, and habits may be similar, but on the inside they are leagues apart. One is dominated by guilt, introspection, and the need to achieve to gain worth. The other is a response to the unconditional love and acceptance of God.

Superficial solutions sound so good. They seem to help so many people. But in the long run, quick, easy answers only prolong and exacerbate the problems of codependency. Real answers are needed that speak to the real issues of worth and identity. These solutions should be experienced during a long process so they will sink in deeply and profoundly. In the next section of the book, we will explore our identity in Christ and the profound impact of healthy relationships in the healing process. We will also continue to learn how to identify codependent behavior, how to maintain objectivity, and how to make good, healthy decisions.

Summary

Hurt and Anger

1. Why is there so much hurt and anger in a codependent's life?

2. What are some reasons why we try to obstruct pain and control anger?

3. Do you see any of the following in your friend or relative's life? If so, describe in detail...

   a) Numbness:

b)   Pain without gain:

c)   Excusing the offender/blaming yourself:

d)   Displaced anger:

e)   Outbursts of anger:

f)   Using self-pity and anger to manipulate others:

4.   Are you afraid to face hurt and anger in your life? Why, or why not?

5.   In what ways does he avoid responsibility for mistakes by blaming others instead of admitting his own errors? Why do you think he does this?

6. Who or what can help him to be honest and express his pain in a safe environment?

Guilt

1. Explain why codependents so often feel guilty:

2. What are some of the differences between *the sorrow that produces a repentance without regret* and *the sorrow that produces death*?

3. Do you see any of the following aspects of guilt in your friend or relative's life? If so, describe how these affect his self-concept and his relationships.

   a) Guilt crushes:

   b) Guilt motivates:

c)   Introspection:

d)   Comparison:

e)   Guilt makes you crazy:

f)   Using guilt on others:

4.   What would his life be like if he had a strong sense of worth and were not plagued by guilt?

Loneliness

1. Why does a person who devotes himself to rescuing and serving often feel lonely?

2. How does a lonely person think and feel about himself?

3. How does he think and feel about others?

4. What are some reasons why many of us feel that taking the risk of self-disclosure and intimacy is too great?

5. In what ways does your friend or relative feel:

   a) Abandoned by people?

b)   Abandoned by God?

c)   Abandoned by authority?

6.   What facades does he use to keep people away? What are the results of using these?

The Codependent Christian

1.   What things does your friend or relative feel that he has to do as a Christian to feel better about himself?

2.   What are some ways that the Scriptures can be misapplied to feed codependent behavior?

3.   How does codependency affect:

a)   His view of God?

b) His identity and worth?

c) His relationships with others?

d) The standards and rules he sets for himself?

4. What are his dominant motivations for obedience?

5. What are some superficial solutions you can think of (such as: "Just pray about it," or "Spend one hour with the Lord everyday") for codependency?

6. Why don't these superficial solutions work?

Chapter 5

The Process of Healing for a Codependent

I asked Sharon a couple of questions: "How would you describe yourself? What adjectives would you use?"

Sharon thought for a minute, then she said slowly, "That's hard for me. I guess I'd say: warm, outgoing...things like that."

"What else?"

After a long pause, she said, "Stupid, ugly...I hate the way I look! I hate the way I act! I hate everything about me!" Sharon put her head in her hands and cried. Her identity, her self-concept, and her sense of worth were clouded and darkened by her codependency. Her inner feelings were quite different from her outer demeanor.

As we have seen, codependents have been deprived of a sense of value. The unconditional love and acceptance they need has been withdrawn to some extent, and they attempt to get worth by rescuing, helping, pleasing, and being successful. But no matter how well they perform, these solutions only give short-term satisfaction.

Healing, growth, and change in a codependent's life occurs most effectively in the powerful blend of learning to *experience* the love and power of God. This takes place in the context of strong, honest, affirming *relationships*, through a patient and persistent process. Psychologists call this a *psychodynamic process*. The apostle Paul described it long ago in his letter to the Ephesians:

> *As a result, we are no longer to be children, tossed here and there by waves, and carried about by every wind of doctrine, by the trickery of men, by craftiness in deceitful scheming;*

> *But speaking the truth in love, we are to grow up in all aspects*
> *into Him, who is the head, even Christ,*
> *From whom the whole body, being fitted and held together by*
> *that which every joint supplies, according to the proper working of*
> *each individual part, causes the growth of the body for the building*
> *up of itself in love.*
>
> Ephesians 4:14-16

The three primary and three corollary characteristics of codependency (introduced in Chapter 1) give us a window to see how codependency affects a person's sense of worth and prevents the process of maturity. Let's take a brief look at these again in this context.

Primary Characteristics of Codependency

Lack of Objectivity—Codependents are so busy rescuing or withdrawing that they don't see the truth about their lives and circumstances. The truth seems too painful to cope with, so they continue to try the same old, ineffective, and painful solution: pleasing others to gain their love.

A Warped Sense of Responsibility—Codependents play the roles of savior and/or Judas, either rescuing to earn a sense of value, or withdrawing to avoid the pain of rejection and failure.

Controlled/Controlling—A codependent is like a puppet, doing whatever others want him to do. He tries desperately to please them while he also tries to control his own life so he can avoid failure. in addition, he tries to control others so they will contribute to his success and ability to win approval.

Corollary Characteristics of Codependency

Hurt and Anger—Codependents feel hurt when they are condemned, manipulated, or neglected, and become angry with the one who hurts them.

They repress these painful emotions, only to have them emerge in the form of displaced anger, disproportionate anger, or depression.

Guilt—If someone attempts to get worth from being good and pleasing people, then any failure—or even perceived failure—leads to intense pangs of guilt. Codependents are ashamed of themselves. They are driven to do better, to do more, and to analyze every thought, emotion, action, and relationship to see if they can improve.

Loneliness—Since codependents desperately want to be loved, they try to make others happy, successful, and feel good. But even when others seem to like the codependent, he still lives in fear that he might do something they might not like. His fear of letting them down causes him to live with loneliness.

This review of the identity of a codependent reminds us that his sense of value is based entirely on his ability to perform and please others. His perspective is deep and strong, but it leads only to more pain, more obsessive-compulsive behavior, and more emptiness. It is a false hope. However, the Scriptures give us another solution.

Biblical Identity

How would you respond if someone asked, "Who are you?" We usually think of our identity in terms of our function in society, so you might say, "I'm a salesman," "I'm a mother of three boys," "I'm a lawyer." Or you might say you're an American, a Republican, a Democrat, or a Christian.

When the apostle John wanted to identify himself in his Gospel, he did so relationally. He called himself "the disciple whom Jesus loved" (John 13:23; 21:7, 20). John's sense of being loved and accepted by Christ was so strong that this was how he referred to himself.

When the apostle Paul wrote to the churches, he also put a great deal of emphasis on identity. As a general rule, the first half of each letter is about the identity of believers; the second half, specific applications of that identity. His circular letter to the Christians in Ephesus is particularly instructive. Let's take a look at part of the first chapter:

*Paul, an apostle of Christ Jesus by the will of God, to the saints
who are at Ephesus, and who are faithful in Christ Jesus:*

*Grace to you and peace from God our Father and the Lord
Jesus Christ.*

*Blessed be the God and Father of our Lord Jesus Christ, who
has blessed us with every spiritual blessing in the heavenly places in
Christ,*

*Just as He chose us in Him before the foundation of the world,
that we should be holy and blameless before Him. In love*

*He predestined us to adoption as sons through Jesus Christ to
Himself, according to the kind intention of His will,*

*To the praise of the glory of His grace, which He freely bestowed
on us in the Beloved.*

*In Him we have redemption through His blood, the forgiveness
of our trespasses, according to the riches of His grace,*

Which He lavished upon us...

*In Him, you also, after listening to the message of truth, the
Gospel of your salvation—having also believed, you were sealed in
Him with the Holy Spirit of promise,*

*Who is given as a pledge of our inheritance, with a view to the
redemption of God's own possession, to the praise of His glory.*

Ephesians 1:1-8,13-14

This passage clearly relates to our identity. Let's look more closely at
several of the key words.

Chosen—Verse four states that as believers, we have been chosen by God.
But why did He choose us? Because we are smart, good-looking, rich, efficient,
or worthy in some other way? No, we have been chosen so that we can be
declared holy and blameless before Him—not perfect in our behavior, but secure
in our identity.

One of the ways I like to communicate this sense of being chosen to my
children is to ask them: "If somebody lined up all the little girls and little boys in

the whole world and told me that I could pick one of each, do you know who I'd choose?"

Catherine and Taylor usually smile and say, "Who, Daddy?"

I wave my finger around the room like I'm surveying the millions of children in the world, then I quickly point to them and say, "You, that's who I'd choose. Do you know why?"

They grin and ask, "No, Daddy. Why?"

"Just because I love you." They really enjoy my doing this, and I think it communicates to them how very much I value them.

Adopted—Verse five states that we, as Christians, have been adopted by God. We usually use the term "child of God" without thinking about it, but He didn't have to adopt us. He could have let us remain helpless and hopeless people. He could have made us His slaves. He could have obliterated us in His righteous wrath. But He didn't. He adopted us like the Romans adopted a person— as an adult child with full privileges as an heir. A good illustration of this is in the movie *Ben Hur*. As a slave, Judah Ben Hur was adopted by the Roman admiral, Arias. He was granted full sonship, given a ring to signify his place in the family, and accepted and loved by Arias.

Forgiven—As Christians, we have been forgiven (v. 7). Christ's death is the complete payment for our sins. The wrongs that condemn us as guilty before God have been paid in full. We are not simply excused as our sins are waved off by a benevolent grandfather figure. Those sins demand payment, the awful payment of Christ's death on the cross. To what extent are we forgiven? The verse tells us, "according to the riches of His grace." No sin is too great, no offense too bad (except refusing to accept Christ's payment for sin).

Sealed—The seal of Rome (v. 13) signified ownership and security. When Christ was put in the tomb, the Pharisees asked Pilate to make it secure so no one could steal the body and say that Jesus was raised from the dead. Matthew's Gospel records Pilate's directive:

> *Pilate said to them, "You have a guard; go, make it as secure as you know how."*

And they went and made the grave secure, and along with the
guard they set a seal on the stone.

Matthew 27:65-66

The seal of Rome was the ultimate in security, yet it could not prevent Christ from being resurrected.

Paul used the concept of a seal to express the believer's security in Christ. The Holy Spirit's seal is the ultimate in spiritual security, but unlike the Roman seal, it cannot be broken. This seal signifies that we have been bought by the blood of Christ (1 Corinthians 6:19-20), so we are owned by God. It also means that we are secure in our relationship with Him. If we have trusted in Christ as our Savior and have experienced His forgiveness and adoption, then He will never drop us, lose us, or reject us.

Paul wrote to the believers in Rome:

I am convinced that neither death, nor life, nor angels, nor
principalities, nor things present, nor things to come, nor powers,
Nor height, nor depth, nor any other created thing, shall be able
to separate us from the love of God, which is in Christ Jesus our
Lord.

Romans 8:38-39

We are secure because we have been sealed by the Holy Spirit. But codependents don't feel secure. In fact, they seem to have a consistently inaccurate view of God. In our book, *Your Parents and You* (Rapha Publishing/Word, Inc.), Robert McGee, Jim Craddock, and I explain that a person's view of God is shaped by his relationship with his parents. In codependent, dysfunctional families, children grow up with a distorted view of God. If parents are abusive, children will probably believe that God is harsh and condemning. If parents are neglectful, children will probably believe that God doesn't care about them. Similarly, spouses of compulsive persons can allow their marriage relationship to adversely influence their view of God.

But the clear teaching of Scripture is that God is not like anybody or anything! He is far more loving, powerful, kind, strong, and concerned about us than we can imagine.

This is one of the painful ironies of codependency. God is the only consistent, loving One whom people can always count on for unconditional love, acceptance, wisdom, and strength. Yet He is seen through a codependent's distorted lenses as harsh, mean, demanding, and distant. We need to remember that it took years for the codependent to develop that misperception, and it will also take time for him to develop a correct perspective.

Codependent Christians are hindered in their spiritual maturity and their experience of the love and power of God. We have seen how codependents value the approval, affection, and respect of people because they believe such affirmation will give them the security and worth they long for. Spiritually speaking, they are guilty of the same sin the Pharisees committed. Jesus reproved the Pharisees because *they loved the approval of men rather than the approval of God* (John 12:43). I don't mean to be too harsh, but we need to call this practice what it is: *idolatry*.

Any time a person tries to get security and value from someone or something other than the Lord, it is idolatry. The attempt to control other people or secure power and approval by serving involves putting oneself in God's place. The surrender of manipulative control and the acceptance of God's grace are central to the Christian faith. Yet as we have seen, the codependent usually tries to control his own life and the lives of others. He doesn't want to give up control. He wants *more* control. Codependents almost always serve others to control them and gain power and approval. Such service is idolatrous.

As codependents recognize their propensity to gain worth by pleasing people (especially that *certain* person), they may be overwhelmed with the depth of that tendency in their lives. It may seem impossible to change. But encourage them to hang in there! Objectivity is usually painful, but the Lord is a kind and patient Master. He knows their past and He knows their pain. Help your codependent friend or loved one learn to see God as a kind and gentle Father who will provide all the encouragement, strength, and time that is needed. Overcoming a lifetime of idolatry is tough, but it is possible. Codependents can be free! As their identity and view of God begin to change, they will have an increasing sense that God does indeed care about them deeply, that He is trustworthy and that He has a wonderful plan for their lives.

As codependents begin to apply these truths in a relationship of love and affirmation, they sense the light and salt of Christianity. In this context, they learn to face the truth about themselves, God, and others. They learn that they have only limited responsibility in the lives of others. They learn to have their own desires and dreams, and they learn to let other people make their own decisions. They learn to be honest about emotions: their pain of rejection, intense anger, and disappointments, as well as their love and hope. They learn that it's OK to fail, because their sense of worth is not threatened by failure. They learn to try for the right reasons. And finally, they learn to love and be loved, to be honest with people, and to give and receive in relationships.

Find a Friend

A person cannot overcome the grip of codependency alone. Even though he might learn some valid information and apply some of what he learns, at a certain level of his life, the deception and lack of objectivity within him are too severe to fight the battle alone. His thought patterns are too ingrained and his habits too well established. He needs the honesty and encouragement of another person before he can make substantial progress. He needs to see someone else model self-worth that comes from the Lord and the freedom and motivation that can be experienced in a Christian life.

Though this level of friendship is rare, some people will be able to provide a spiritually healthy environment for the codependent's growth. He should *not* settle for another codependent who needs someone to need him! He should not look for someone to rescue him! Instead, he needs a mature individual who can do four things: (1) affirm him, (2) encourage him, (3) be honest with him, and (4) be a good model for him. Let's look at the importance of each of these responsibilities.

Affirmation—God's love and acceptance of us is based on *His* grace, not on *our* goodness. Throughout the Scriptures, our identity is explained in terms of who we are.

Codependents who obtain identity based only from their ability to perform and please people (and who come up short!) sometimes have a difficult time believing they can be accepted for just who they are. It may take a while to believe and experience that degree of affirmation, but it is vitally important to their growth and development.

Encouragement—A spirit of encouragement is closely linked to affirmation. This concept is demonstrated by a coach on the sideline, cheering on his players. "You can do it! Don't stop now! Cut to the left! Now pass the ball!" He can't go in and take the place of any of the players, but he gives directions as he communicates confidence in them. Over the course of a season or two, the players develop both skill and the confidence that they can execute the plays needed to win.

I have several people who play the "coach" role in my life, but none as much as my wife, Joyce. Whenever I am discouraged, she communicates confidence in me. Whenever I need some fresh ideas, she usually has plenty of them. When I'm heading in a new direction, she asks me questions I haven't even thought of, so I will be more aware of opportunities and pitfalls. Whenever I need someone to believe in me, she is there.

All of us need somebody, or several somebodies, to give us that combination of direction, feedback, and confidence that leaves us feeling encouraged.

Honesty—Most codependents have repressed deep hurts and anger for years. These emotions surface from time to time, but not in healthy, constructive ways. They get depressed for weeks, or they explode in anger over something relatively small. They need a friend who will let them express their emotions and thoughts in a safe environment, without fear of being ridiculed for feeling and thinking the way they do. They need people who won't give simple answers like, "Just pray about it," or "Boy, you need to confess that and move on," or "Give thanks in all things, then don't think about it again." Such advice may be a well-meaning admonition, but it only encourages more repression.

Exposing accumulated hurt and anger is usually a very messy process. As Todd began to see how his parents' divorce had made him an overly-responsible rescuer, he determined to stop rescuing his mother. It didn't quite work out that neatly, however. When he told me about his last encounter with his mother, he was angry. "I saw it coming—the self-pity, the threat of rejection—and I didn't want to rescue her. But I did it again!" Though he hadn't eliminated the problem, Todd's honesty gave us a chance to talk about the situation.

Modeling—Reading books, going to classes, and listening to tapes can be helpful, but people's lives are changed most effectively by seeing an example of someone who has dealt with the problem and is now living a well-adjusted life. As in every other aspect of life, emotional and spiritual health is "caught, not taught." Codependents need to spend time with healthy people in healthy situations. They need to see real emotions expressed and real solutions found for real problems. Phoniness and superficial answers won't cut it! Rescuers need to observe objective people responding to their own successes and failures, and those of others, in as many different situations as possible: job, family, recreation, church, etc.

This is the pattern Christ established in His relationship with His disciples. They were with Him almost constantly for more than three years. They observed Him in the good times: healing the sick, giving sight to the blind, raising the dead, and speaking to the multitudes at the height of His popularity. They must have had incredible discussions as they walked along and gathered around the campfires so many times. They also saw Christ respond to hard-hearted legalists as they condemned Him. They saw Him experience ridicule, and they observed Him weep at unbelief and death. They watched Him agonize in prayer over His impending torture and execution. And finally, they saw the risen Christ in His glory before He ascended into the clouds from a hilltop outside Jerusalem. They saw Him in every conceivable situation!

Obviously, codependents won't find any models like that! But for those of us who know codependents, our challenge is to be people they can watch and learn from, people who are honest about the struggle of life, and people who are faithful to trust God rather than relying on our own capabilities.

The Process of Emerging from the Eclipse of Codependency

Almost twenty years ago, Elisabeth Kübler-Ross wrote a book (*On Death and Dying*) about the process that terminal cancer patients experience after their condition is diagnosed. She identified a pattern of five phases that the patients would undergo: (1) Denial, (2) Anger, (3) Bargaining, (4) Depression, (5) Acceptance.

The process of coping with physical disease closely parallels that of dealing with emotional difficulties. Let's go through each of these stages in terms of dealing with our codependent friends. I have made a couple of modifications to the Kübler-Ross model. First, I will put Bargaining before Anger. Most of the codependents I have talked with are primarily concerned with how to get parents, spouse, etc., to love them. Any anger they feel is still mixed with the hope that the loved one will finally change. When they finally give up on swapping something to gain love, then their anger is usually more focused (though not necessarily more intense).

Another change I have made is the label of the fourth stage. I will use "grief" instead of "depression." It seems to me that "depression" has a very negative connotation based on the fact that the source of depression is often repressed anger. "Grief" connotes a more positive and healthy perspective on this part of the process.

So as we go through the Kübler-Ross stages (with slight alterations), we will look at: (1) Denial, (2) Bargaining, (3) Anger, (4) Grief, and (5) Acceptance. These phases do not constitute a push-button, 1-2-3 kind of process. A person may move quickly through one phase, but very slowly through another. And he may go back and forth, re-entering a stage he has already gone through as he becomes aware of other pains and hurts not previously seen. Generally speaking, however, a person will not progress to the next stage until he has more or less fully experienced the one he is in. The following diagram may be helpful. Objectivity is the door which opens into the process. Acceptance is the door leading out of it and into health. In the middle are three vats, or containers, representing bargaining, anger, and grief. A person will not progress to constructive anger until he is through with bargaining, and he will not experience grief until he has spent his anger. (This, of course, will not mean that the person does not experience mixed feelings during each phase. It only means that one emotion will be dominant during that period of time.)

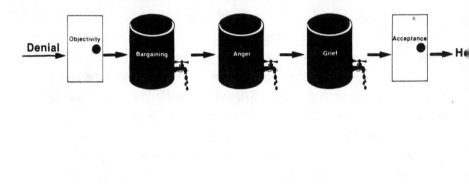

Denial

Previous chapters have devoted a good deal of space to denial, so we will briefly recap some of the reasons why codependents live without objectivity.

- Codependents think their families, circumstances, thoughts, emotions, and behavior are "normal." They don't have a model of healthy behavior with which they can contrast their pathological codependent behavior.
- Codependents may have developed an unconscious defense mechanism of staying so busy that they don't have time to reflect and feel pain. Many are driven to accomplish their own goals and those established by organizations, corporations, and others. This compulsion is a vain attempt to block pain and gain a sense of self-worth.
- Some codependents become passive and emotionally numb in their effort to block pain. They avoid decisions and relationships when the risk of

failure and rejection seems too high. (Most people use some combination of compulsion and passivity in their attempts to cope with codependency.)

• Some codependents are so crushed, hopeless, and depressed that they don't believe anything good will ever happen to them. They withdraw into a cocoon of morbid introspection and self-hatred.

• Some codependents have been sheltered from the pains and joys of life. Often they are prevented from experiencing success or failure because of overprotective parents.

• The pain of neglect or condemnation is so great for some people that they recoil at being loved by someone. "Affirmation hurts. Love is painful. I can't take it!" said one sad woman.

• Some codependents have repressed so much hurt and anger that they lose their tempers fairly often. These explosions are unlike the productive expressions that we will examine later (in the "Anger" section). At the Denial stage, such outbursts are not the product of understanding and objectivity. The anger is just the "tip of the iceberg," and is coupled with guilt and self-hatred. Some people see their anger and think, *I must be pretty far along in the process.* But in reality, they haven't even started the process because they have yet to see the root cause of their anger.

No problem can be resolved if it is denied. Objectivity is the door which enables codependents to begin the process of healing. Understanding the pathology of codependency and seeing its cumulative effects can be shocking at first, but that realization is necessary before a person can participate in the rest of the process.

Bargaining

When a person first begins to recognize the effects of codependency in his life, he will often respond by trying to bargain with himself, his family, and God. Christy learned about dysfunctional families from a close friend, and quickly saw those painful effects in her own life. At the end of the conversation, she blurted out, "Then how can I get my father to love me?" Her friend explained,

"That's the wrong question, Christy. It's not up to you to get your father to love you. *He* is responsible for that. It's up to you to become independent and secure in the Lord, whether your father ever loves you or not."

Bargaining takes many shapes and forms, but its goal is to get other people to change. Usually the codependent will first offer some change in himself.

I'll be a better husband to her. I'll spend more time with him. I won't nag him anymore, then he'll love me the way I want to be loved. I'll keep the house clean. I'll get a job. I'll be more affectionate.

People can come up with all kinds of "deals" to get others to love them. Bargaining is not the objectivity that codependents lack. In spite of the apparent give-and-take, bargaining is still a desperate attempt to somehow get a person who has hurt the codependent deeply to give him the love that he craves.

Believing the best of others is *usually* good and right. It is *usually* a virtue. But when the other person has proven after months and years of irresponsible, manipulative behavior that he is pathological, then believing the best of him is *not* a virtue. It is naive and foolish. It is the haven of denial.

Bargaining is an expression of hope. The codependent hopes that the other person will change and provide the love and worth that is needed. But it is a false hope. The hard truth, based on the reality of objective observation, leads us to a painful but honest conclusion. The codependent needs to let go. He needs to abandon the vain hope that the other person will change. Letting go doesn't sound very spiritual, but it is. Letting go is a reflection of reality. It is an act of abandoning the idolatry of pleasing others and being accepted by them as the way to win self-worth. Actually, it is an act of worship to the Lord.

When the codependent gives up and stops bargaining, he looks the truth in the face. At that point he may become very angry with the one who has lied to him, used him, and hurt him so deeply.

Anger

Anger is a difficult issue to write about. By its nature, it is volatile and consuming. Many people hold strong (and often contrasting) opinions about it.

Treatments of anger are frequently superficial, and sometimes complex and confusing.

All anger is not wrong, nor is all anger right. In some cases it is good and wholesome, but many times it is sin. There is a difference between feeling angry and acting angry. It isn't wrong to feel angry as a natural response to some type of pain or injustice. When people see this type of anger as sin, they may either deny that it exists or express it indirectly and inappropriately (passive aggression).

The active expression of anger can be from either righteous or unrighteous motives. It can either hurt or heal. If feeling anger prompts someone to stop being manipulated, to become independent of others, and to communicate clearly instead of withdrawing or attaching, then the response to that feeling is good and healthy. If, however, feeling anger prompts revenge and/or withdrawal, then the response is destructive. Two classic passages about anger are Ephesians 4:26-27 and James 1:19-20.

Paul admonishes us to *feel* angry, but not to express anger unrighteously:

> *Be angry, and yet do not sin; do not let the sun go down on your anger,*
> *And do not give the devil an opportunity.*
> Ephesians 4:26-27

> *James warns us not to let our expression of anger hurt others:*
> *Let everyone be quick to hear, slow to speak and slow to anger;*
> *for the anger of man does not achieve the righteousness of God.*
> James 1:19-20

We can differentiate between destructive anger and constructive anger. Destructive anger is based on the desire to harm another person. It consists of outbursts, rage, seething, and revenge. Constructive anger occurs as the result of being harmed by another, yet prior to any destructive response. Too often we cross the line so quickly that constructive anger immediately becomes destructive. That's why Paul wrote, *Be angry* [constructive anger], *and yet do not sin* [destructive anger].

Most of us have mixed perceptions about anger. If we have repressed it for a long time, it may surface in embarrassing ways. So we rationalize it. We feel guilty about it. We ignore it. We hate ourselves for it. Consequently, most of us either consciously or unconsciously come to the conclusion that anger is wrong.

In the process of emotional healing, a codependent may try to skip from "Bargaining" to "Grief" because grief seems more acceptable. But he won't be able to thoroughly grieve until he comes to grips with the reality of his anger.

Couependents have difficulty with anger because current offenses are compounded by a backlog of repressed anger at past offenses. The instruction in Ephesians to not let the sun go down on their anger has been disregarded so many times that denial and repression have become the normal way of dealing with anger. The person cannot be expected to dredge up every offense of the past and deal with them all in a day. It takes longer than that! After a period of honest reflection and truthful expression of repressed emotions, the codependent is *then* able to deal effectively with each offense as it occurs.

Perhaps a diagram will help describe how repressed anger makes it difficult to deal effectively with present offenses.

The response to a new offense is complicated and compounded by a backlog of past offenses. Most of us either repress our anger at the new offense, too, or respond in anger that is disproportionate to the offense.

Through being honest about repressed anger and expressing it in a safe environment, the backlog is gradually diminished.

Eventually, our backlog of anger is expressed and dealt with. Because new offenses are not complicated by repressed anger, we can respond more objectively with appropriate anger and forgiveness (Eph. 4:26-27).

In the unconditional love and acceptance of God, each person has an environment in which he can be honest and vulnerable. He not only can acknowledge present hurt and anger, but he can also be objective about the cumulative hurts of the past—and the resulting anger that has been stored inside. David instructs us to be open and honest with God because He cares for us:

Trust in Him at all times, O people; pour out your heart before Him; God is a refuge for us.

Psalms 62:8

The writers of the psalms certainly felt free to express anger honestly. In Psalm 88, the author complains that he has been forsaken by God:

I am reckoned among those who go down to the pit; I have become like a man without strength.

Forsaken among the dead, like the slain who lie in the grave, whom Thou dost remember no more, and they are cut off from Thy hand.

Thou hast put me in the lowest pit, in dark places, in the depths.

Thy wrath has rested upon me, and Thou hast afflicted me with all Thy waves.

Thou hast removed my acquaintances far from me; Thou hast made me an object of loathing to them; I am shut up and cannot go out.

Psalms 88:4-8

In Psalm 109, David expressed his anger toward those who had hurt him deeply.

They have also surrounded me with words of hatred, and fought against me without cause.

In return for my love they act as my accusers; but I am in prayer.

Thus they have repaid me evil for good, and hatred for my love.

Appoint a wicked man over him; and let an accuser stand at his right hand.

When he is judged, let him come forth guilty; and let his prayer become sin.

Let his days be few; let another take his office.

Let his children be fatherless, and his wife a widow.

Let his children wander about and beg; and let them seek sustenance far from their ruined homes.

Let the creditor seize all that he has; and let strangers plunder the product of his labor.

Let there be none to extend lovingkindness to him, nor any to be gracious to his fatherless children.

Let his posterity be cut off; in a following generation let their name be blotted out.

Psalms 109:3-13

Many codependents screech to a halt at this phase of the healing process because they have developed an aversion to expressing anger—especially about the person who has offended them the most. Unless this impasse can be broken, they cannot proceed to grief and acceptance, or ultimately to stability and health. Here are a few reasons people refuse to become angry:

- Some believe all anger is wrong and sinful. *If I am angry, then I must be a bad person.*
- Some believe if a problem exists in a relationship, they must be at fault! In their lack of objectivity, they feel a misguided, blind loyalty to the one who has deeply hurt them. This loyalty is coupled with pangs of guilt at even the thought of being angry with him or her.
- Some excuse any offense. "Oh, that's OK. I don't mind. It doesn't hurt me. I'm used to it by now, and besides, she couldn't help it."
- Some are afraid of the backlash of anger—rejection, ridicule, withdrawal, and/or wrath of the offender.

- Some are afraid that if they experience healing, warmth, and intimacy in the relationship, they will be hurt all over again. The risk is too great.
- Some consider being angry an option they will not even consider. Seething anger and bitter hurt are repressed. In their denial, these codependents won't acknowledge any problem at all.
- Some have been taught by trusted Bible teachers that their parents or spouse is an authority figure to whom they must unconditionally submit. In a dysfunctional family, such submission is used to manipulate or condemn the codependent.

It is very important for codependents to find a safe environment of unconditional love and acceptance where they can honestly express the cumulative effects of repressed anger in their lives. They need friends who will provide both affirmation and correction. Exposing hurts and anger can be awkward and difficult, and it will take time. However, at the heart of this constructive anger and pain is a sense of stability that is based on objectivity. Even though it can be tremendously painful to express these emotions, the codependent is still likely to experience a sense of satisfaction in discovering why he has struggled so much for so long. Yet after his anger is expressed, he will likely feel a sense of loss.

Grief

"There is a little girl in me who was never loved by her father," Susan said sadly, "and she never will be."

Will said, "I had such hopes and dreams for our marriage, but now it will never be what I had hoped. I feel so empty."

"Our darling little girl was so cute, so loving," Margaret said, as she remembered her daughter. "But drugs have ruined her life...and almost ruined ours, too. We'll just have to make the best of it now."

When the vat of anger has been drained to a trickle, a sense of loss begins to dominate the codependent. He grieves as if someone had died. Indeed, it seems as if *he* died. His system for feeling worthwhile, harmful though it was, has been taken away. Or he realizes that he has wanted something—love and acceptance from a certain person—very badly, but may never have it. He wanted intimacy, warmth, and laughter, but now he feels only hurt and emptiness.

Janice was progressing through this process, and she described her grief to me: "I was sitting in church one day and I had the strangest feeling. I felt like I was going to cry and throw up at the same time. I thought, *I'm losing it! I'm really going crazy!* After the service, I realized that I was grieving. I guess I've bottled up my emotions for so long that they came out in a strange way."

Over the next several months, Janice continued to grieve. She felt sad. She felt lonely. But she also knew that this was a part of the process. She really wasn't going crazy—quite the contrary. She was becoming healthy!

How should a person grieve? How long? Good questions, but there are no clear and simple answers. Nor are there formulas for grieving. A person grieves by giving himself the freedom to feel loss for as long as it takes. It helps greatly to have someone to affirm him and provide perspective as he goes through this process. (Does this sound like a broken record?) He needs someone who will listen to him and comfort him without giving quick and easy solutions to make him feel better.

Months may go by. Emotions will fluctuate. Sometimes the person will feel the catharsis of the healing process, but sometimes he will feel very sad. He may become emotional over things that never affected him before—an act of kindness, a crying child, a new offense. All such behavior is normal and healthy. It is part of being a real person with real feelings in real relationships. The Lord will provide grace and comfort. In time, the person will be able to accept all that has happened to him.

Acceptance

Denial has been overcome. Bargaining has taken place. Anger has been exposed and expressed, and the grieving process is coming to an end. The process was painful, but now the person is objective about life: its good and bad, its righteousness and wickedness. He is no longer comfortable with simple, easy answers. He has discovered that they just don't work.

The codependent gains a new depth in his relationship with the Lord and with other people. He discovers new perspectives on life, new values, and new lifestyles. He doesn't feel driven to accomplish every goal because He has a new set of priorities. He enjoys a healthy blend of independence from others and a new dependence on the Lord. He can say no, and he can admit being wrong.

People who see their lives objectively can help others be objective, too. Their perceptions are wise, and they can comfort hurting people because they understand their hurts (2 Corinthians 1:3-5).

Mark asked, "When I get to the "Acceptance" phase, will I experience total freedom? Will I be completely free from the effects of my codependency, or will I always be scarred?" I thought for a minute, then I told Mark about an incident in my life years ago.

When I was young, our family bought some Roman candles to shoot on New Year's Eve. My father lit them and off they flew into the night, exploding in all kinds of colors. I had been parked under the arm of my mother on the front steps, but lighting the fireworks looked like lots of fun. After my father lit another one, I ran down the steps and grabbed it. I held it straight up, waiting for it to blast into the sky. Instead, it backfired inside the sleeve of the winter jacket I was wearing!

Like it was yesterday, I vividly remember looking through sheets of tears at my parents. They grabbed me and took me inside to see how badly I was hurt. It was worse than they could have imagined. At the hospital, they learned that I had third-degree burns over most of my forearm.

For the next several months, the burn required almost constant attention: wrapping, unwrapping, putting on medicine, making trips to the doctor, crying in the night. My exuberant little sprint to grab the Roman candle had resulted in agony for the whole family. But after a few months, scar tissue began to form and gradually the burn required less and less attention.

Today I still have a sizable scar on my arm, but I rarely think about it until I see someone staring at it when I'm wearing a short-sleeved shirt. Though the scar remains, the pain has been gone for years, and the consuming attention it required is just a memory.

Codependents have deep wounds that require a lot of attention for a while. Even the emotional bandaging and medication seem to hurt. But with loving treatment, scar tissue will gradually form as the healing process continues. Though the scar may remain, the pain will gradually be replaced by healing and health. The process isn't pleasant, but it is essential if the wound is to heal.

Summary

Biblical Identity

1. Before you read this chapter, what adjectives would you have used to describe yourself?

   What adjectives do you think your friend or relative would use to describe himself?

2. Paraphrase these passages:

   a) Romans 3:21-26

   b) Colossians 1:19-22

c)   1 John 4:9-11

d)   1 Corinthians 6:19-20

e)   Romans 8:1

f)   1 Peter 2:9-10

g)   2 Corinthians 5:20

3.   In what ways does his life (attitudes, thoughts, actions, relationships, etc.) reflect that he believes these passages? In what ways does his life indicate that he doesn't really believe them?

4.   Describe his relationship with his parents (include both its positive and negative aspects):

5. How have these relationships affected his view of God?

6. Why have his attempts to try harder and please people more not given him a strong sense of worth?

7. Does the idea of "peeling the onion" in applying these truths encourage him or discourage him? Why?

8. Whom do you know (an individual or a group) that can help him in the healing process?

Find a Friend
1. What might or might not happen if your friend or relative tries to deal with his codependency alone?

2. How can a you, a group, or a counselor help him? Be specific.

3. Make a list of people, groups, and qualified counselors your friend or relative can select from.

Emerging

1. Why do we try to bargain to get people to love us?

2. Why is bargaining a false hope? Why is it important to give up?

3. Describe the differences between destructive and constructive anger:

4. What are some ways a person can deal with a backlog of repressed anger?

5. Look at the reasons why many of us won't or can't be honest about our anger. Do any of these apply to your friend or relative? If so, which one(s)? How will understanding this roadblock help him?

6. What might grief be like and feel like for him?

7. What are some changes that might happen in his life when he gets to the acceptance phase?

8. Which phase is he in now? How can you tell?

9. What (or whom) does he need to help him through this process?

Chapter 6

Essential Elements in the Healing Process

In trying to understand codependency and its effect on your friend or loved one, the last chapter may have seemed a bit negative. The process of going through anger and grief stages is not pleasant, though it is necessary. But as a codependent learns more about how he has been affected by dysfunctional relationships, he also learns how to respond in new and more positive ways. These new responses are characterized by three essential steps: identifying, detaching, and deciding.

First, he can identify improper behaviors, feelings, thoughts, words, and actions that have become habits of codependency. Then he can detach and reflect about how he can stop responding in his usual way, and respond instead in a positive, healthy way. After his reflection, he can decide on a course of action. And this time his response will be based on objective reality, not on codependent reflexes.

Identify. (See it.) Detach. (Analyze it.) Decide. (Choose a response.) This is the path to freedom and health. In this chapter we will examine these three actions. First, we will discover how to identify codependent behaviors.

Identifying

As a codependent rescuer learns more about his identity in Christ, and as he sees the patterns of codependency in his life, he will be able to identify many of the specific codependent things he says and does. He will also be able to see some specific characteristics of codependency in others.

For some people, identifying codependent behavior will be fairly easy: "Oh yeah! I've done that for years!" Others will have a harder time identifying those behaviors as they recognize a few instances but can't see the patterns very clearly. Still others lack objectivity to such an extent that they don't see *any* characteristics of their codependency. Healing can't begin for these people until the Holy Spirit begins to overcome their denial.

Identifying codependent behavior is the trigger mechanism necessary for objective reflection, and ultimately for living in freedom and godly independence. Before this realization occurs, however, most people think their situations are normal.

Dysfunctional behavior destroys objectivity. As codependents compare their lives to that of the alcoholic, drug addict, perfectionist, workaholic, bulimic, sexual abuser, or whoever in the family is "really messed up," they think they're doing pretty well. They fail to recognize that exaggeration, guilt, loneliness, being manipulated, manipulating others, and outbursts of anger are signs of relational pathology, not normalcy. They are unable to see the devastation in their own lives (which are *not* "normal") because of their inability to face reality.

Many codependents truly believe that they are terrible people (though they try so hard to help), and that the offending person in their lives is wonderful (though he manipulates them through guilt, self-pity, anger, and fear). Other codependents rationalize that they are very good people with no wrong motives or hidden faults.

The strength of this deception is so great that at one point, a young man I know told me he didn't think he had ever sinned. Yet at other times in his life, this same man was overcome with guilt and morbid introspection. He couldn't evaluate his life in terms other than black-or-white.

As you have been reading about these many examples of codependent behavior, they serve as red flags. You might think, *That's my friend (or spouse)! That's what he does!* Or *My wife does that to me!*

Or *I respond that way to my husband.* Try to think beyond a few particular events and identify any deep-rooted patterns that may exist.

One man told me about his relationship with his codependent, condemning, manipulative father. He said, "I've been angry with my father several times, so I guess I'm pretty objective." This man couldn't see the pervasive insecurity and myriad of defense mechanisms he had developed during his life. We must be more honest with ourselves. We need to identify both the patterns and the specific events that make up those patterns.

We have examined a number of common codependent feelings and behaviors. Now, to facilitate the action of *identifying* such behavior, we will divide these feelings and behaviors into the "savior" and "Judas" categories (previously discussed in Chapter 3). Think of the codependent person in your life. Which of these, or variations of these, can you identify in his or her feelings, attitudes, and behaviors?

Savior	Judas
Feelings: grandiose importance, superior, certain, euphoric, confident, appreciated, angry, self-righteous, jealous, possessive, easily hurt	**Feelings:** depressed, lonely, angry, helpless, confused, fear, hurt, inferior, hopeless, guilt, numbness, trapped, martyr, persecuted, lethargic, worthless, shame, tired
Thoughts and Words: *It's all your fault.* *You made me fail.* *I can help.* *He (she) needs me.* *Why aren't people as perceptive as I am?* *I deserve their respect and love.* *I can make life good.*	**Thoughts and Words:** *It's all my fault.* *I'm a failure.* *I can't do anything right.* *Everything I do is wrong.* *Yes,* but I mean *no.* *No,* but I mean *yes.* *I don't deserve their respect and love.* *Life will never be good for me.*
Black or White: *People really need me.* *I am indispensable to the kingdom of God.* *People won't be helped and the Great Commission can't be fulfilled without me.*	**Black or White:** *People really need me, but I'll only let them down.* *Good Christians wouldn't think or act this way.* *God must be mad at me. He'll punish me.*
Actions: exaggerate (high), self-promotion, overcommitted, workaholism, easily manipulated, control others through praise and condemnation, rescue people without being asked, deny reality, compulsion to avoid failure, giving, helping, try to please people, defensive, overly responsible, outbursts of anger, rationalizes, trusts self and others	**Actions:** exaggerate (low), self-denigration, withdrawal, avoid people and risks, easily manipulated, control others though self-pity, deny reality, passive-aggressive, afraid to fail, believes he can't please anybody, defensive, irresponsible, outbursts of anger, rationalizes, doesn't trust self but may trust others

Identifying codependent behavior may seem like a cognitive exercise, but it usually elicits a flood of emotions as a person begins to realize how deeply he has been affected. There is both bad and good news in this realization. The bad news is: What he sees is probably only the first layer of the onion. As he deals with the hurts, fears, anger, and habits there, yet another layer will be exposed. Don't get discouraged. He needs to face reality no matter how difficult it is. The good news is that hope is readily available. The Lord can provide wisdom and strength to enable us to deal with a codependent relative or friend.

Detaching

When Joyce and I bought our house in Austin several years ago, the tree in the front yard (which in Central Texas, we were privileged to have!) was in a slightly peculiar position. Its roots were a little exposed on the downhill side, so I decided to build a rock wall around that side with the rocks left over from building the house.

It was my first attempt at masonry. I bought some cement and sand, and passed on buying a trowel when I learned it would cost almost seven dollars. That seemed too steep a price to pay for such a small job.

I mixed the cement in a big trash can and proceeded to lay the rock and cement, smoothing the mortar with my hands. Three hours later, I had almost finished the wall. It was a lot harder than I had thought it would be!

For twenty or thirty minutes during this time, I had noticed a tingling sensation in my fingers, but thought it was just because my hands had been wet for so long. When I washed off my hands with the hose, I was shocked to see that the skin on the ends of my fingers was gone in several places! There were deep holes! I quickly finished the wall and went into the house to see the extent of the damage. It was, I learned, a case of concrete poisoning.

I had to put antibiotic cream and band-aids on the ends of my fingers for almost two weeks, and today there are scars on those fingers. One of the amazing things about this incident is that there was so little warning, so little sense of "something's wrong!" Only when the wounds were exposed was there a realization of the damage. Then healing could begin.

This story is analogous to codependency. When a person finally observes the damage that has occurred in his life, he may be shocked by its extensiveness. It takes time and attention for healing to take place. So often identifying the damage, he should reflect on the best course of action.

Codependents are trained to react, *not* respond. They instinctively rescue, withdraw, or attack. They feel the compassion of a rescuer, and they feel anger, hurt, and self-pity. This instinct is deeply ingrained, but it needs to be changed. They need to detach—to separate themselves from that codependent reaction system in order to think, feel, and reflect. They also need to detach from the people who have controlled them.

Detachment requires time, objectivity, and distance (emotionally and/or physically). Circumstances vary so widely that it is impossible to provide a formula for detaching. But it will help if the person asks himself: *What do I need (time, space, objectivity) so that I can reflect honestly on this situation?*

Sometimes a person can identify, detach, and decide in a heartbeat. This is especially true when he has had practice in this process. But usually he needs to remove himself from the offending person or situation before he can be objective. The pressure of close proximity is simply too strong. He should go to another room, take a drive in the country, go away for a weekend, or do whatever is necessary to feel and think. A distraction may help him acquire a sense of calm before a period of reflection. He might read a book or magazine, watch a television show, take a walk, or do whatever helps him.

Some psychologists use the word *detach* to describe the act of isolating oneself from others in a negative, harmful way. In contrast, codependent literature uses same the word to describe a positive, healthy action—stepping back to obtain objectivity about a person or situation. Detachment is not the same as withdrawal. Withdrawal is a defensive reaction to block pain and avoid reality. Detachment has the opposite goal: to become objective, deal with reality, feel real emotions, and determine the best course of action.

The Scriptures have a lot to say about reflecting on reality and truth so that we can respond wisely instead of reacting codependently. We are instructed to take the time necessary to acquire such wisdom.

Acquire wisdom! Acquire understanding! Do not forget, nor turn away from the words of my mouth.

Do not forsake her, and she will guard you; love her, and she will watch over you.

The beginning of wisdom is: Acquire wisdom; and with all your acquiring, get understanding.

Proverbs 4:5-7

As the codependent learns to detach in order to be honest about his feelings and objective about his circumstances, he will see a more defined contrast between codependent and healthy thoughts, feelings, and actions. Perhaps it would be helpful to list some questions to ask during the period of detachment. Here are some suggestions to get the person started.

- Why did he say (do) that to me?
- What did he mean?
- How do I feel about it?
- How might someone else feel?
- Is he controlling me? Condemning me? Neglecting me?
- Why do I feel guilty? Driven? Afraid? Lonely?
- Am I rescuing?
- Am I acting as a savior? A Judas?

It might also be helpful for the codependent to develop some statements that trigger certain thought processes in his mind. This may seem "hokey," but getting a handle on objectivity is very difficult for codependents. He should use whatever helps him! Here are a few statements that may be useful.

- I'm not responsible for making him happy.
- I'm not responsible for fixing the problem.
- He needs to be responsible for himself.
- I can respond calmly.
- I can say no.

- I can say yes.
- I can make my own decisions.
- I feel angry...lonely...guilty...driven...afraid.
- I am loved, forgiven, and accepted by God through Jesus Christ.

When a person detaches and becomes objective, he is able to admit how he feels. He can be angry, sad, glad, or afraid in a safe environment. He becomes able to consider his options, make the best choice, and act in confidence.

When the person isn't sure of what to do, or when he feels pressured to react, he often uses evasive language. A good friend of mine nailed me on this. Michael and I spent a lot of time together several years ago in Missouri. One day, another person asked me if I wanted to go to a party. I really didn't want to go, but I wanted to be polite. (Actually, I wanted to avoid offending the person and, therefore, avoid rejection.) So I said, "We'll see." Mike piped up and said, "When Pat says, 'We'll see,' he really means no." Touche! I would have been a lot better off if I had just learned to let go of my codependent behavior.

"let go"

to "let go" does not mean to stop caring;
it means I can't do it for someone else

to "let go" is not to cut myself off;
it's the realization that I can't control another

to "let go" is not to enable,
but to allow learning from natural consequences

to "let go" is to admit powerlessness—which means the outcome
is not in my hands

to "let go" is not to try to change or blame another;
it's to make the most of myself

to "let go" is not to "care for," but to "care about"
to "let go" is not to judge, but to allow another to be a human being

to "let go" is to not be in the middle, arranging all the outcomes, but to allow others to affect their own destinies

to "let go" is not to be protective; it's to permit another to face reality

to "let go" is not to deny, but to accept

to "let go" is not to nag, scold or argue, but instead to search out my own shortcomings and correct them

to "let go" is not to adjust everything to my desires, but to take each day as it comes, and cherish myself in it

to "let go" is not to criticize or regulate anybody, but to try to become what I dream I can be

to "let go" is to not regret the past, but to grow and live for the future

to "let go" is to fear less and love more

Deciding

It is possible to detach, to feel, to think, to consider options, but then to be immobilized and not make any decision at all. After a period of detached reflection, the person needs the courage to act in positive, healthy ways. He needs to stop rescuing and controlling, and start saying and doing those things that reflect independence, security, strength, and health. This is extremely important, both for his own sake and for the sake of those he typically rescues and controls.

In this section, we will examine a process for taking steps toward emotional and relational health. The process has four components: making independent choices, setting limits, surrendering control of others, and enjoying life.

Making Independent Choices—Several months ago, I received a call from Sheila, the booking agent of a music group we had contracted to perform at a conference. We had worked out the contract months earlier, at which time the group had agreed to obtain their own housing. Now, Sheila explained, "We really tried to get housing for the group, but we just couldn't find any. You'll have to get it for us."

The more we talked, the more pity I felt for Sheila and the group. I could feel pangs of guilt as I wrestled with saying no. Our budget was tight, and I knew we couldn't afford to pay for their housing. We wouldn't have agreed to the contract in the first place if we thought we would have to shell out money to house everyone. But my desire to rescue and my sense of guilt won. Instead of saying no, I said, "I'll see what I can do," and hung up the phone.

I sat in my office and stewed. I wasn't angry with Sheila. I was angry with myself. I had done it again! I had rescued instead of being objective.

I took a few minutes to think about what had happened. I tried to sort out the facts objectively, and then I realized that we couldn't provide the group's housing. We could take their housing costs out of their fee, or they could find their own housing. That was fair. It was objective. It was right.

I called Sheila and told her I had reconsidered the situation, and then explained my decision. I wasn't angry. I understood their predicament. But my decision was the right one. It wasn't my responsibility to take the time or spend the money to provide housing for the group.

Sheila was a little surprised that I called back so soon, but she said she understood. In a week or so, she had worked out the details, and everything was just fine. Because I had *identified* a codependent tendency and *detached* myself long enough to regain my objectivity, I could then *decide* what was best.

Making independent choices requires making honest statements and not using evasive language or double-talk. It is saying what we mean and meaning what we say. It also means that we can do helpful things for people because we want to, not just because we will feel guilty if we don't.

My wife and I recently had a normally hectic morning getting the children ready for school and preparing for a staff meeting at home. Joyce came down the stairs with two heaping baskets of dirty clothes. As she weaved her way through the breakfast room and kitchen on her way to the garage (a.k.a. laundry room), I stopped her. "Wait a minute," I said, "I'll get that for you." As I took the baskets, a friend who was early for our staff meeting asked me, "Pat, are you rescuing Joyce, or are you helping her because you want to?"

I stopped to think about it. Then I said, "No, I'm doing this because I want to. She could do it herself, and that would be OK. I don't think I would have felt guilty if I hadn't carried the baskets."

Ah, the freedom of making independent choices: doing right things for right reasons!

The key to making sound, independent decisions is asking and determining the answer to this crucial question: "Lord, what do You want me to do?" A codependent usually assumes that the Lord expects him to rescue and control others. He feels guilty if he doesn't do absolutely everything he possibly can for people. And often, he feels guilty even though he does.

Seeking God's direction is still valid for the codependent, but his mindset needs to change. That's the purpose of detaching. We shouldn't assume that the Lord always wants us to rescue, help, and/or control people. His primary concern is that we renounce the idolatrous behavior of trying to please others in an attempt to gain security and worth from them instead of from Him. When we are independent from the control of others, we become open to the Lord's wisdom and direction. Only then can we be objective about the question: "Lord, what do You want me to do?"

Codependents normally take responsibility for others but not for themselves. (The first time someone told me this, I thought he was crazy. I saw myself as a very responsible person. I didn't realize I expected other people to make me happy while I felt responsible for making them happy.) They need to take responsibility for their own lives, with the Lord's direction and strength. If they have been passive, they need to take steps of action. If they have been driven, they need to learn to say no to some things, even if other people don't understand or approve. If they have been saviors, they need to let others experience the consequences of harmful behavior. If they have felt like a Judas, they need to build their confidence by focusing on the unconditional love and acceptance of Christ. If they have acted like children, they need to start acting like adults.

Each person should take steps to be responsible for his own life and honor the Lord in his personal relationships, goals, and habits. He should develop a healthy independence from the bondage of pleasing others and a godly dependence on the love, wisdom, and strength of the Lord. This process begins when he asks the crucial question, "Lord what do *You* want me to do?"

Setting Limits—After learning to make independent choices, the next vital part of healthy living is recognizing limitations and setting realistic limits in relationships with others. This is where the concept of "staying on your own ranch" (introduced in Chapter 2) becomes essential. My friend, Mark Baker, says that every person is given a piece of land when he is born, but a codependent allows people to take water from the property, cut down its trees, and trample its pasture. He even encourages people to take advantage of his land, all in the hope of winning their approval. But after his house has been burned, his crops and pastures trampled, and everything stolen, he finally gets angry and determines to set limits. At first, he determines not to let anyone even set foot on his property. He guards it with his rifle to be sure no one takes advantage of him again. After he has rebuilt his home, planted new crops, and become established again, he will become more willing to let people on his land. But even then, he will ensure that others do not take advantage of him.

The codependent has very few limits. He feels responsible and guilty for everything. He tries to help everybody. But as his sense of identity, independence and objectivity grows, he will quickly realize that he can't continue life without limits. He needs to set limits clearly and firmly, such as:

- This is what I will do. This is what I won't do.
- I will not take this kind of behavior anymore.
- I'm not responsible for his happiness.
- I refuse to be manipulated.

- I'm sorry, I wish I could help you, but I can't.
- Why did you say that to me? Do you know how I feel when you say things like that?
- I don't want to talk about this.
- I want to talk about this.

And, instead of anticipating his needs and jumping in to rescue him, you can listen patiently and wait for him to ask for your help. Then, you can make a decision about whether or not to help.

"But this seems so selfish!" some codependents might say about setting limits. "They need me! What about being a servant and going the extra mile?" Again, the question is: What is a rescuing, compulsive, codependent reaction to others' needs, and what is a healthy, independent, loving response? Inherent in this compulsive sense of being needed is the idea that *It's all up to me, and if I don't help, who will?*

Can the Almighty, Omnipotent, Sovereign Lord take care of that person the codependent is so determined to rescue? Is the codependent so indispensable that he takes the place of God? He may, indeed, be hindering the other person's development of responsibility and independence by continually rescuing him. And he may also be blocking the other person's, as well as his own, dependence on God to provide and protect. It's not up to him! The Lord can take care of that person, and He can take care of the codependent as he learns to identify, detach, and objectively decide to set limits that restrict compulsive rescuing.

Stop Controlling Others—Just as a person seeks to make his own independent decisions, he should give other people the freedom to do the same. A codependent can learn to calmly and clearly let people know what the consequences of their decisions will be. It's fine to love and encourage them, but they also need to know that their choices make a difference. Instead of yelling or withdrawing, a codependent can learn to say something like, "That hurt me a lot. If you say things like that to me, it will hurt our relationship"; or, "If you continue to treat me that way, I don't want to see you"; or, "Until you have proven that you are responsible, I won't trust you to do this or that."

Calm, loving discipline is much different from codependent manipulation, allowing the other person to develop much needed responsibility and learn the consequences of his own behavior. The pattern of controlling with praise and condemnation, anger and withdrawal, and overt expressions or subtle gestures is frequently used with children. It works most of the time, but the intensity is usually raised as the child tests limits and gets used to each new level of manipulation. The attempt to control him through praise and condemnation may prevent his ability to see situations clearly and make objective decisions. And in adulthood, he will probably treat his children the same way. The cycle will then continue.

Some of the consequences of codependent living are difficult, both for the rescuer and the person he is trying to help. Years of alcohol or drug addiction can result in the reality of financial collapse. Bitterness, manipulation, and lying often result in broken relationships and estrangement. The emotional trauma of guilt, hurt, anger, and loneliness are deep wounds that aren't easily mended. There are no quick and easy answers to these problems, but codependents can pick up the pieces, find a friend to help, and trust the Lord to give them a fresh start.

Enjoying Life—After learning to make independent choices, set limits, and give up trying to control others, enjoying life is the fourth component in the process of developing emotional and relational health. As a person grows in independence and objectivity, he will begin to feel free and spontaneous. Instead of being driven to please others—and often being disappointed by their response— he will begin to experience unconditional love from God and from a new set of friends. He will begin to enjoy life—*really* enjoy life!

Many of the things that seemed so desperately urgent will fade in their importance. Love, intimacy, spontaneity, and new goals and dreams will take their place. The perverted self-denial that characterized life will change to healthy giving and receiving. One man told me that anytime he was offered something, even ice cream, his first response was to refuse it.

"Why?" I queried.

"I don't know," he said. "I guess I just didn't think I was worthy of receiving a gift or having fun."

Now, this man is learning to value himself, to give freely, and to receive with freedom and gratitude. He's beginning to enjoy life.

What would your codependent friend or loved one enjoy? What has he withheld from himself because he deems himself unworthy? What goals and dreams can replace the driven and compulsive desires of codependency? What can he do this week (today!) just for the fun of it? Give him some ideas: Go out to dinner. Buy a game. Go to a movie. Buy a canoe. (I did!) Take a vacation. Tell a joke. Laugh. Help somebody because you want to. Dream new dreams. Make new friends. Relax. (If relaxing sounds like prosperity theology or blatant hedonism, it's not. Encouraging a guilt-ridden, overly responsible person to relax and have some fun is meant to give balance and health to his life, not to promote hedonism.)

I heard a pastor tell a story that relates to this new, independent life a codependent can have. The pastor described his lawn in Southern California. In the summer, the oppressive heat bakes the grass, and it begins to turn brown. Months go by with very little rain, then the Santa Ana winds bring more heat in the late fall. By mid-winter, the yard looks barren. Not a green blade can be seen anywhere. The flowers have wilted long ago. The lawn is lifeless...or so it seems.

Then, in the spring, the rains begin. At first the lawn looks like a large mud puddle, but after a couple of weeks, a few sprigs of green begin to appear out of the muck. Then, almost overnight, the grass sprouts and spreads very quickly. There is life again!

Many codependents are like that yard in mid-winter. They feel emotionally, spiritually, and relationally dry and barren. They have not seen much sign of life for a good while, and they've just about given up hope. When the refreshment of encouragement and objectivity comes their way, the grip of codependency doesn't give up easily. Change cannot be detected for a while. Then a few sprigs of new life appear, and then a few more. As the rains continue, a full lawn will replace what was barren ground only a short time before. At long last the person experiences the greenness of hope, life, depth, intimacy, reality, and love!

As your friend or relative *identifies* his unusual codependent reactions, *detaches* himself so he can feel and think clearly, and then *decides* to act courageously, he will begin to experience this kind of transformation. It may be slow at first, but with the encouragement of a friend, and the love and power of God, it will happen!

Summary

Identify

1. Has your friend or relative thought of his family as "normal"? Is it? Why, or why not?

2. Take some time to identify codependent behavior in your friend or relative's life. Be as specific as possible as you describe your feelings, thoughts, statements, and actions.

Detach

1. What does it mean, to detach? Why is it important to detach?

2. What are some similarities and differences between withdrawing and detaching?

3. Describe some of his usual codependent responses in regard to the following:

    a) Feelings:

    b) Thoughts:

    c) Actions:

4. Does he want you to help him detach? How do you know?

5. If so, what questions and statements can help him detach?

6. What are some realistic expectations as he learns to detach (time, consistency, etc.)?

Decide

1. Name some differences between codependent and independent choices:

2. Does your friend or relative want you to help him make decisions? How much help is too much interference, control, and rescuing? How much is just right? How can you tell?

Section 2

Understanding Yourself

You may be reading this book for a number of reasons. Perhaps you simply wanted to find out a little more about codependency. The goal of Section 1 was to provide some basic information on this emerging and widely relevant topic. But more than likely you know someone who is displaying codependent behavior. Section 2 is designed to help you see where you fit in the picture: How do you relate to your codependent friend or relative?

Chapter 7

Your Relationship to the Codependent

You may be the codependent's parent, child, spouse, sibling, friend, neighbor, employer, employee, or whatever. But certain aspects of the relationship may not be easily understood. Those aspects include your attraction to the rescuing behavior of the codependent, your role in shaping his controlling and rescuing tendencies, and your responsibility in his healing process.

If you are not a relative of the codependent, it might be instructive to reflect on how you got into the relationship. Are you a close relative? Were you placed with the other person because of your employment? Did you move into the neighborhood and develop a friendship with a person who is a rescuer? Or did you choose the relationship? Could it be that you are attracted to this person because you enjoy being rescued? Are you a needy person who appreciates the attention and empathy the codependent gives you?

It will prove to be very difficult to help the codependent person through the healing process if you reinforce certain aspects of his or her overly responsible behavior which you like, while you attempt to change the aspects you don't like.

The nature of the relationship is an important factor in determining the level of responsibility you have in the codependent's progress. Each person, regardless of the relationship, needs to set limits on his responsibility. (Remember, the codependent needs to learn to be responsible for his own life!) But a close family member will have more inherent responsibility than a casual friend.

An even more important aspect of the relationship is the emotional impact which you and the codependent have on each other. Some people can have a very positive, healing effect. Others may have a quite devastating effect on the codependent's emotional stability and health.

In the rest of this chapter, I want to describe several broad categories of people and how each of these relates to someone who struggles with codependency. Some of the things I will bring up in this chapter are very painful and may even reveal that your role has been quite detrimental in another person's life. My goal in this chapter, however, is understanding—not condemnation.

We will examine broad categories of relationships involving a codependent: (1) the addictive or dependent person; (2) the absent or neglectful person; (3) the abusive person; (4) another codependent; (5) other kinds of hurting people; (6) someone who is in the middle of gaining health and stability, and finally, (7) a relatively healthy, secure person.

This chapter is not intended to be a comprehensive analysis of family systems. It is only a cursory glimpse at some of the issues and complexities in these systems.

You May Be an Addictive Person

As we saw in Chapters 1 and 2, the characteristics of codependency were first identified while observing the families of alcoholics and then drug addicts. As families of other addictions (sex, work, food, gambling, success, etc.) were carefully studied, it was noted that the addicted person provided a perfect environment for the cultivation of hurting, controlling rescuers.

Some addictions are fairly easy to identify by outsiders (though denial mechanisms in the families are often so strong that neither the addicted person nor his family admit to a problem). But some problem behaviors are not usually identified as addictions. For example, someone who is addicted to work may be applauded by peers and promoted by his employer because of his "dedication to the job." Conversely, people who are addicted to sex or gambling may be so discreet about their compulsions that no one close to them even knows about it for years. While addicts may sometimes be compulsive and overly responsible in some areas of life, they *all* tend to be irresponsible in their relationships. They often need to be rescued, but then resent the rescuer's intrusion in their lives.

Scott's mother was addicted to prescription drugs. His father couldn't take the strain, so he hid at work 70-80 hours every week and stayed busy on weekends. The mother was taking uppers every morning and afternoon, and downers to enable her to sleep at night. Gradually she became more tolerant of these drugs, taking stronger dosages and then stronger prescriptions. Her wide mood swings and volatile behavior kept Scott in constant fear. He never knew where he stood with his mother. Scott's sister became rebellious and left home in her mid teens, but Scott tried a different tactic to soothe the pain and gain some acceptance: rescuing.

Scott became so perceptive about his mother's moods that he learned to anticipate her wants before she ever voiced them. She, in turn, learned how to pull his strings with praise, condemnation, and neglect. He became a puppet. He began to feel what she wanted him to feel, say what she wanted him to say, and do what she wanted him to do. He almost completely lost his own identity as he became enmeshed in his mother's emotions and lifestyle.

Another disorder with different overt signs but similar effects on others is experienced by a dependent person. This person isn't an addict by definition, though he *is* addicted to being helped by others. He is dependent on others to make decisions for him, to help him express his feelings and, generally, to function in life.

Sara is known as a "really nice person" whose children "take good care of her." She always has a kind word for people and everybody enjoys seeing her at church or shopping. Her closer friends, however, see her from a different perspective. One person first suspected she was a codependent since she expected others to rescue her so often, but then it was observed that Sara wasn't actually a rescuer. She was simply dependent on certain people. When Sara's mother came for a visit, several friends heard her say, "Sara is such a sweet person, but you know, she has never had much sense. Why, all her life I've had to make decisions for her. She never even knew how she felt if I didn't tell her!"

In such an oppressively controlling and degrading environment, Sara had developed into a very dependent person. Her children had learned to "take good care of her" by rescuing her.

You May Be an Absent or Neglectful Person

The addictive or dependent person is *obviously* needy, so he promotes rescuing behavior in others. Absent or neglectful people are also needy, but their need isn't as obvious because they're not around very much. Divorce is the most common reason for a parent being absent (though some divorced parents maintain very close contact with their children). Similarly, parents or spouses who immerse themselves in work and/or travel, sports, committees, campaigns, and other activities don't relate to their families in a way that builds emotional and relational strength.

Another form of emotional neglect occurs when someone is still in physical proximity with others but withdraws to the newspaper, magazines, books, or TV for inordinate periods of time. This is a common defense mechanism to avoid the risk of intimacy or the pain of rejection.

Neglectful or absent people don't cultivate rescuing behavior in others as readily as addicts because the needs are not as obvious. The incidence of codependency is still, however, quite significant in these families.

Rob's parents were divorced when he was four years old and his older sisters were seven and six. His father remarried and moved to another state across the country. Rob rarely had any significant contact with him. His mother was forced to work and often came home too emotionally and physically exhausted to give Rob the attention and affection he needed. His grandmother was a wonderful and kind woman, but Rob's sense of need compelled him to develop an overactive responsibility to take care of his mother—and win the love from her that he so desperately wanted.

Rob's mother was *not* a dependent person who wanted to be rescued by her son. She was simply a burned-out woman who couldn't cope with the physical and emotional stresses of being a single mother with three children. Yet this environment still promoted rescuing tendencies in Rob.

You May Be an Abusive Person

You may have inflicted emotional, physical, or sexual abuse on someone. Physical, sexual, and verbal abuse create tremendous stress in people's lives. It has terrible effects if it happens at work or in the neighborhood. It is awful if it happens to a spouse, and even more tragic when children are the victims. Adults usually have at least *some* capacity for objectivity or help from other people, but children generally believe their parents are omnipotent, omniscient, and omnipresent. They have nowhere else to go for objectivity and encouragement. When parents are abusive, children absorb all of the pain and anger that is communicated to them.

In addition to the bonding problems which develop in children (and even those who are abused as adults), abused victims may also develop a propensity to control the out-of-control people and situations. Self-protection may drive them to "live on others' ranches." They try to make others happy to eliminate the abuse and take care of them in the hope of being appreciated. All the while they deny the reality of their pain and anger as well as the pathology in the relationship. Conversely, other abused people may overreact in the opposite direction, becoming withdrawn and indecisive, and avoiding contact (or at least conflict) with others at all cost.

One woman had a verbally abusive father and a dependent mother. She developed a rigid system of obedience to try to do everything just right so her father wouldn't yell at her. She became very controlling of herself, her mother, and the entire family, hoping she could fix everybody's problems and keep her father calm and happy. That was the theory, but it didn't work out that way. Even after years of trying to control herself and others, she never saw her father change. Yet she still tried controlling and rescuing to solve the problems in her life. She saw no other alternative.

Another woman who was sexually abused developed an eating disorder. Her unhealthy attachment to food was an attempt to have some sense of identity. She also tried to control her husband and children through self-pity. Abuse creates tremendous longings, attempts at escape, and methods to control and rescue in order to lessen the pain and win approval.

You May Be Another Codependent

Two codependents...two needy people controlling and rescuing each other, living on each other's ranches and both expecting to be cared for by the other. Both wonder what the other person is thinking and feeling, but neither one is honest about his feelings and desires.

They experience wide swings in their emotions. Sometimes both are in the savior mode and it's a power play to see who can control and rescue the other. Often one is up and the other down, so they neatly fall into the pattern of rescuer and rescuee. Sometimes they are both down, expecting to be rescued, and both become bitterly resentful that the other is "so selfish."

One dad in a double codependent father/son tandem controlled his son by being extremely demanding. He would be harsh, but became a velvet brick as he said gently, "Son, I only give you my advice because I really care about you." The son couldn't take his father's fierce disapproval. After repressing tremendous inner anger, he meekly did whatever his father wanted.

A rescuing parent, child, sister, brother, or close friend may believe that he is utterly indispensable to the codependent. "No one cares about him the way I do. What would happen to him if I didn't help him?"

The two people in the relationship play mind games, guessing what each other wants or needs, giving advice that isn't solicited, and taking charge of each other's lives without any real communication ever taking place! Each may think he knows how the other feels and what he needs without ever asking his opinion or—heaven forbid!—letting him decide for himself.

This relationship develops into a Jekyll and Hyde, love-hate arrangement. Each may temporarily appreciate being rescued and cared for by the other, but will deeply resent any intrusion or manipulation sooner or later.

You May Be Another Hurting Person

How's this for a broad category!? Many hurting people (such as the lost child) are not rescuers. These people do, however, often enjoy being rescued by a codependent, so they gravitate toward attentive, caring, fixing, people.

This category of people may have some type of emotional disorder, but they don't venture onto anyone else's ranch. Each lives on isolated parts of his own ranch because he has given up other portions of his ranch to the aggression and control of others. Some of these people live in a nicely decorated little cottage with all the flowers blooming out front and the walls freshly painted. But the picket fence around their house is the entire scope of their domain because an abusive parent has created in them a deep fear of failure and rejection. Others are so deeply hurt that the only part of their ranch left is an old dead tree. They're hiding on one of the limbs as the vultures circle overhead! These are needy people, and they are often glad to have someone care for them—even if that person is a little controlling in the relationship.

The relationship goes along pretty well as long as the codependent is in the savior mode. Then there's an eager rescuer and a willing rescuee. But when the rescuer wants to be rescued, he can be bitterly disappointed if the hurting person doesn't reciprocate.

Ben and his wife, Teri, exemplify this kind of relationship. Ben is a classic codependent. Teri appears to be a very confident and capable person, but she is really insecure. Ben does a lot for Teri, most of which he enjoys because Teri appreciates his attention and caring so much. Yet pressure points develop quite often. Sometimes Ben feels used. Often he feels that if he doesn't rescue Teri, she will express her disapproval by withdrawing from him. Sometimes she resents his overresponsibility as an intrusion on her turf. Sometimes Ben hurts, expects Teri to take care of him, and becomes angry if she doesn't show the same empathy and active care he has given her. But Ben and Teri never talk openly about their real feelings and thoughts. That's too threatening to them.

You May Be a Codependent in the Stages of Growth

People who have been in the recovery process for a while often provide the greatest motivation for a codependent just beginning the process. These people don't yet "have it all together," but they have two outstanding characteristics. First, they understand what's going on in the codependent's life. They know how deceived, hurt, and manipulated he can be. They know how hard it is to take those first steps. In short, they empathize. And second, they are usually enthusiastic about their own progress. The wide mood swings have smoothed out a little. They are more realistic about the process and encouraged that real changes are taking place in their lives and relationships. Often these people provide the level of encouragement necessary to get the codependent on the road to growth and health.

Suzanne felt tremendous stress in her relationships with her family. Her mother was an alcoholic who expected to be catered to. Her father was passive. Her husband expected too much from her. When she had two small children who needed her time and attention, her stress level went on overload. Her coping mechanisms of rescuing, controlling, and making others happy were no longer working. She couldn't cope anymore.

Months ago, her friend Betty had told her about a book on codependency. She wasn't interested then, but she was now. She called Betty about the book, read it, and was utterly confused. Did Betty think that book applied to her? Maybe there *were* one or two things....

Suzanne and Betty met several times to talk about their codependency. Betty had been meeting with a group of women for about seven months to discuss the topics in the book. She was excited about her own progress and understood Suzanne's reluctance to admit to her codependency. "I remember when somebody first talked to me about this stuff," Betty told Suzanne. "I thought she was nuts! But as she kept talking about her own life, I started seeing some of those same things in me—like sometimes how quick I am to change my opinions to suit other people while at other times I'll defend my opinions to the death! Both extremes are defenses."

Suzanne was slow to recognize those things in her own life, but she couldn't deny that Betty was really growing—and that Betty cared about her. Over the next few months, a few lights started coming on in Suzanne's mind. She started seeing what Betty had been talking about, and she joined the weekly discussion group. They continued their progress together.

You May Be a Relatively Healthy and Secure Person

You may be a friend, pastor, or counselor with a healthy family background, or someone who has worked through your own hurts and fears to a significant degree. You may be a family member who has had the courage to get involved in the recovery process and work toward healthy, growing relationships. You are well aware of the pain and deceitfulness that is deep inside you, but you can be honest about life and experience the freedom and direction that healing can bring. Your life is more or less characterized by:

- objectivity about your own life and the lives of others
- expressing love without controlling the person
- respecting your own growth process and the growth of others

A codependent may not initially gravitate toward a person like this. A healthy person doesn't show overwhelming, obvious needs that a rescuer needs to fulfill. Also, a healthy person doesn't respond as readily to the controller's attempts to manipulate. Honesty and objectivity are threatening to the codependent who is used to the game of "Don't trust. Don't feel. Don't talk."

But as the rescuer becomes aware of the nature of his codependency, he will begin to see that a relatively healthy person is a tremendous, God-given resource for him. By modeling honesty and health, by communicating with love and gentleness, and by encouraging the codependent to be responsible for only his own decisions and feelings, the more stable person can have a powerful and lasting impact on the codependent's life.

Summary

This brief glimpse at different categories of people may have revealed some issues you need to work through before you focus on helping a codependent overcome his problems. The next chapter will briefly outline the necessity of resolving personal needs as a part of the process of helping others. Before you go to Chapter 8, answer the following questions with your codependent friend or relative in mind:

1. Which of the types of relationships best fits the relationship you have with your codependent friend or relative? Why?

2. What are some characteristics of your relationship?

3. How do each of these characteristics affect you and your relationship with him or her?

Chapter 8

Your Needs

At this point you might be thinking, *I thought this book was about the codependent's needs. Why are we wasting time looking at my needs?* Perhaps an illustration will help explain.

Brad's wife has the classic characteristics of codependency. Connie is from an alcoholic family. She sees herself primarily as a savior, but drops into the depression of feeling like a Judas from time to time. She has been successful at manipulating Brad as well as her mother and some others by using either self-pity, sarcasm, or outright condemnation. Brad has recently been reading up on codependency, but when he tries to talk to Connie about it, she gets very defensive.

As Brad explained all this to me, he was desperate. He wanted some stability in his marriage. He wanted Connie to stop being so controlling and defensive. He leaned forward with a look of intensity, hurt, and fear on his face and asked, "What can I do? How can I help her?"

Before talking to him about Connie, I asked Brad a few questions about himself. We talked about his parents and brother. His father was a hard-working man who was also very involved at church and in politics. Brad's mother stayed busy around the house. Their family times were pleasant, but infrequent. His brother was eight years older, so they did very little together as Brad grew up. He seemed to have a lonely childhood—not tragic, but without much attention from his family. Then I asked more about his relationship with Connie. "How do you respond when she tries to tell you how you should act or feel?"

"Oh, it doesn't really bother me. I know she's doing it to help."

"How about when she uses self-pity to get you to feel sorry for her?"

"Well, she does so much for people. I guess she has the right to feel sorry for herself once in a while."

We didn't seem to be getting anywhere. There seemed to be a lot of dissonance between the hurt I observed in Brad's face and voice and the calm control expressed in his words.

"Brad, let me give you an observation," I said gently. "Usually, adults who felt left out as a child feel lonely. And people who live with someone who is overly responsible, self-pitying, or controlling feel hurt. You seem to have experienced some hurt and loneliness, both in your family when you were young and now in your relationship with Connie." I waited for a reply.

Brad groped for words, "Yeah...I, uh...uh... I have felt hurt, but, uh... sometimes really hurt...and angry, too, but I don't want to focus on my own needs. Connie is the one who really needs help."

Brad and I had several conversations during the next several weeks. As we talked about his own hurts, as well as Connie's codependency, two principles seemed to emerge: (1) People from dysfunctional families are usually much more deeply affected than they think they are; and (2) Often the best chance our codependent relatives or friends have to get healthy is for us to get healthy ourselves.

This chapter will revolve around these two principles and will focus on *your* relational, emotional, and spiritual needs.

As you look at the profound impact your own sins and the sins of others have had on your life, you may realize that you have more wounds than you thought. You may discover that you have rescuing tendencies in your relationship with your friend or relative, or you may recognize that you tend to withdraw when he needs you. As your needs surface and as you experience real healing, you will be able to do much more than just survive. You will be able to grow and develop in every aspect of your life.

We May Be More Deeply Affected Than We Think

All of us are reminded of the deep and tragic results of the Fall as we get into relationships where there is hurt, anger, and deceit. Some of us think that stable, loving families don't experience any of this pain, but they do. Yet in stable and loving families, people learn to be honest about offenses. They learn to forgive one another. They develop the relational abilities to give and receive love. Healthy families don't escape reality. They teach their children to deal with it honestly.

In the last chapter, you saw a number of categories of people—from severely dysfunctional to healthy—in relationships with others who were codependent. Of those categories, the ones who have learned to be perceptive and honest about life either learned those skills in the context of healthy families (and those are unfortunately few) or started in dysfunctional families but underwent the long and painful process of coming to grips with reality.

Don't forget that people from dysfunctional families usually see themselves and their family members as "normal." They seldom comprehend that their view of God, their self-concept, and their relationships with others are radically affected. Many layers of defense mechanisms are built up to block the pain of reality. It is just too threatening to be objective about the abuse, the anger, the deception, and the hurt.

Even though Brad began to see Connie's codependency, it still took quite a while for him to begin to see that *he* had been deeply affected by his relationship with his parents and his brother. His sense of need and Connie's willingness to meet those needs had attracted them to one another in the beginning. Their deep individual needs then continued to complicate and confuse their relationship.

Over the course of months, Brad and I continued to talk about his family. He began to recall some of the hurt and anger that he had repressed over the years. At first he felt terribly guilty for even entertaining thoughts of anger toward his parents or God. Soon, however, he realized that the psalmists had been completely honest with God, so Brad took the risk of being honest, too. As he did, he began to experience more hope, and he began to relate to Connie in healthier ways. He learned the importance of his own emotional health.

Getting Healthy Yourself

Most of the principles for you to gain relational, emotional, and spiritual health are the same as for someone who is codependent. We will look at these in more detail in the next section of the book, but we will touch on them here. We can describe our needs in a myriad of ways, but these can be put into three related categories: perception, love, and separateness.

Perception—The process of gaining an accurate perception of yourself and your relationships is usually slow, with a few flashes of insight from time to time. Yet after a while, you will develop realistic expectations. You won't expect the process to be over quickly. You won't be as surprised when you see deeper levels of pain or other unhealthy aspects of relationships that have characterized your life. And you will become more comfortable with the complexities of life, not expecting simple answers to explain everything.

Love—Most theologians and psychologists agree that the central need in life is the ability to give and receive love. If you are from a home where people were loved and affirmed, especially if you are from a dysfunctional family and have been in the process of growth for a while, then you probably can appreciate both the need for and the power of love.

In our culture, love has been redefined and reduced to a point that the term usually connotes only a pleasant feeling or sexual attraction. But the biblical description of love is more precise and is explained in three terms.

Eros describes the love of passion, usually between a man and a woman.

Phileo means brotherly affection. It is based on some characteristic of the other person, such as, "I love you because you are pretty (or strong, or smart, or whatever)."

Agape is the term that describes the self-giving, unconditional affection of God (and of God's people). This love recognizes intrinsic value in the other person and continues in spite of his or her performance. It is a commitment to the well-being of another even when it is not pleasant or convenient. Paul described this kind of selfless affection and valuing of others in his first letter to the believers in Corinth:

If I speak with the tongues of men and of angels, but do not have love, I have become a noisy gong or a clanging cymbal.

And if I have the gift of prophecy, and know all mysteries and all knowledge; and if I have all faith, so as to remove mountains, but do not have love, I am nothing.

And if I give all my possessions to feed the poor, and if I deliver my body to be burned, but do not have love, it profits me nothing.

Love is patient, love is kind, and is not jealous; love does not brag and is not arrogant,

Does not act unbecomingly; it does not seek its own, is not provoked,

Does not take into account a wrong suffered, does not rejoice in unrighteousness, but rejoices with the truth;

Bears all things, believes all things, hopes all things, endures all things.

Love never fails.

1 Corinthians 13:1-8a

The love of God is to be imparted by the family, the body of Christ, the Word of God, and the Holy Spirit. People from dysfunctional families, however, often have difficulty experiencing God's love even when they understand it theologically. The family environment is tremendously important. Feeling valued, accepted, and loved is the first critical stage in our development—the bonding stage.

Dr. Burton White has said that children need "irrational love" to enable them to develop a healthy sense of self-esteem. In dysfunctional families, that sense of being valued is, to some degree, impaired. One lady, who was sexually abused as a child, was plagued by intense feelings of self-hatred. The son of an alcoholic realized that his father told him that he cared, but his actions communicated that he really didn't love his son. A young woman realized that she was appreciated as long as she played the role of "the good child" in her family, but the moment she didn't play that role, her parents and brother condemned her until she meekly complied with their demands.

It is easy to see how someone who doesn't feel loved would be attracted to many codependents. The attentive, compassionate codependent gives the hurting person both the time and affection that he craves. But the person often gives up control and self-respect in the bargain because the codependent isn't satisfied with merely providing time and affection. He also wants to control how the other person thinks, feels, and acts. The relationship looks like love. It often feels like love. But it is clouded by the codependent's desire to control.

Again, people from dysfunctional families think their lives are normal. They may think they are experts on the subject, but to some degree, they don't even know what love feels like. If you are from a dysfunctional family, and/or if you have been in a relationship with a codependent for a long time, you need to find a healthy relationship so you can learn to give and receive love. You won't find any perfect people, but you *can* find people who are honest with you, who value you as a person, who are patient with you, and who forgive you when you offend them. In that kind of environment, you can learn to enjoy being yourself.

Separateness—The codependent person in your life has certainly been on—or trying to get on—your ranch. He has been trying to make decisions for you and get you to think, feel, and act the way he thinks you should. If you had developed a healthy independence prior to this relationship, then you probably have been able to maintain a degree of separateness. You have said "no." You have been honest about your feelings. You have chosen to make your own decisions. If, however, you are from a dysfunctional family and you haven't gone through much of the healing process, then you probably have difficulty with separateness—especially now in your relationship with the codependent in your life.

Charles is from a home where his father is a workaholic and his mother is a codependent. His mother smothered Charles with attention—and control. In most of his relationships, especially dating relationships, Charles looked to other people for cues to know what to think and how to feel. When asked a question, he would reply, "I don't know," unless he was absolutely sure that his answer would be accepted. He finally married a woman just like his mother—someone who would live on his ranch and take care of him.

Betty is from a similar family, but responds quite differently. Instead of quickly giving in, she is tremendously defensive. She told me that she feels very guilty when she doesn't give in, but she is so angry when others try to tell her what to do that she refuses to acquiesce.

Charles hides. Betty has her guns blazing! Both have given up most of their ranches. Two codependents sometimes get into a relationship where each one lives on the other's ranch: rescuing, fixing, controlling, and condemning. Each is trying to satisfy his need for love and value by getting the other person to value him. Their relationship becomes almost a game to see who can control whom. Though there may be times of ecstasy, there is often hurt, confusion, and anger. Both desperately want to be loved, but the method used to gain love is to manipulate the other. They both then feel used, not loved. They need the freedom of separateness so they can extend love and let each other make his own decisions.

Separateness, like perception and love, is learned in the context of positive, honest relationships where people talk openly of their hurts, fears, joys, and hopes. If you have been letting others control how you think, feel, and act, or if you feel guilty when you don't let them control you, then you need to get into a relationship with someone who will encourage you to find reality in your life and to help you take the next step. A pastor, counselor, or friend who understands these issues can be of great value to you at this stage.

Summary

In this chapter we have taken only a brief glimpse at your needs. Perhaps you have identified with some of the illustrations of codependency in this book. Or maybe your needs are somewhat different. A few chapters later, we will look at perception, love, and separateness in more detail as we look at the codependent's needs. We encourage you to take plenty of time to reflect on your own family, and other relationships, and then be honest with someone about your thoughts and feelings. Being realistic about your needs and getting into the healing process is the most important thing you can do for the codependent in your life—and for yourself! Before you go to Chapter 9, take time to examine your own family background and needs:

1. Describe your family background. How did (do) your parents relate to each other? To you?

2. What are your needs for perception?

    For love?

    For separateness?

Chapter 9

Your Role in the Codependent's Life

Your role in the healing process of the codependent person in your life should depend on several factors. One consideration is the nature of your relationship, which we examined briefly in Chapter 7. Another is your grasp of the issues related to dysfunctional families, denial, rescuing, and control. A third factor is your ability to listen and counsel. Finally, you must consider your desire to get involved in this process with the codependent.

The codependent needs perception, love, and separateness. If you are experiencing these to a significant degree yourself, then you can play a *primary* role in the other person's development. If, however, you are just beginning to work through these issues, or if you haven't progressed very far in the process, then you should play a *support* role. This role delineation is not meant to be demeaning to anyone. Rather, it is meant to be objective. Certainly a support role is far better than the complicating or damaging role which some people have played in others' lives!

How can you tell if yours should be a primary or a support role? Here are some criteria to consider:

- Are *you* experiencing perception, love, and separateness?
- What is the nature of your relationship with the codependent?
- Do you feel the need for his acceptance and affirmation?
- Are you easily influenced by the other person's self-pity, condemnation, guilt, and enthusiasm?
- Do you tend to be "black or white" in your perspectives of people, especially this person?

- Finally, as you discuss your role with an objective person who understands codependency, what is his advice?

Someone who struggles with codependency needs at least one person to play the primary role in his growth and two or three others to be in support roles. Before we analyze these primary and support roles in more detail, let's look at some general principles that apply to both.

Principle #1: Learn About Codependency

It is important that you understand codependency inside and out. What are its causes? What are the roles in a dysfunctional family? How do rescuing and controlling fit together? Why is objectivity so elusive? Why does someone who struggles with codependency often feel guilty, hurt, angry, and lonely? How does a codependent think and feel? How does progress take place? How do you recognize progress? What are realistic expectations? How do the person's concept of God, self-concept, and relationships change?

Be observant about the other person's demeanor and behavior. His words often say one thing, but his countenance may communicate quite the opposite. Also, complicating factors often have a significant impact on the codependent's life (such as severely strained relationships, dealing with someone's addiction, his own experimentation with drugs or alcohol, obsessive-compulsive behavior, financial problems, difficulties at work, or problems with children). All these factors need to be understood and taken into account as you learn more about a particular person's struggle with codependency.

Quite often, a person in the healing process transfers his thoughts and feelings for someone else (typically a spouse or parent) to the person trying to help him. The helping person or counselor in some way represents the father, mother, sibling, or some other person important to the one being counseled. Such representation can be positive. For instance, a counselee may say to the helper, "You understand me better than my father ever did!" But sometimes this kind of representation is negative.

I once counseled a man who ascribed to me the characteristics of his neglectful father. He became quite angry with me and accused me of not caring for him. While helping another person through the healing process, it is important to expect this kind of behavior. If I hadn't been aware that anger is a common response in these situations, I might have begun to treat him the way his father treated him!

The response by a helper or counselor to the counselee's attitude toward him is called counter-transference. Sometimes the counselor may get caught up in the appreciation expressed by the one he is helping. Other times, he may become angry because the person isn't as responsive as the helper feels he should be. In either case, the helper or counselor has lost some objectivity in the relationship.[1] (For a more complete explanation of transference and counter-transference, see footnote 1.)

Transference on the part of the codependent is normal. It allows the person to feel previously repressed emotions and verbalize hidden fears, hurt, and anger. But if the helper is unexpectedly blind-sided by another's transference, he can react very negatively, short-circuit the process, and damage the relationship. Understanding codependency and the healing process is important for all helpers— primary or support roles.

Principle #2: Listen

In the Book of James, the writer instructs believers to *be quick to hear, slow to speak, and slow to anger* (James 1:19). But few of us have learned to be good listeners even though we live in the "information age." Listening is hard work! It requires that we focus our attention on the other person, not ourselves. And the goal of listening is to understand the other person, not to make sure *we* are heard.[2]

Some of the hindrances to good listening include:

- *Selective listening*—We filter out what we *don't* want to hear and concentrate on the portions of conversation we *do* want to hear. Selective listening is very common in dysfunctional families.

- *Bargaining*—We allow the other person to talk just so *we* can say what we want to. The longer *he* talks, the longer *I* get to talk.
- *Mind-Wandering*—Our eyes look into the other person's eyes, we nod agreement, we empathize with a "Hmmm" from time to time—but we aren't paying attention at all!
- *Escape*–Someone may be pouring his heart out to us. He may be criticizing us. Or perhaps he is simply boring. But all the while we are looking at magazines, reading menus (for the fourth time!), or escaping from the conversation in some other way.

The goal of listening is understanding the other person—not changing his mind. That may or may not come later. First you must be sure you understand him and that he knows you understand. So here are some ideas to improve your listening skills:

- *Ask questions*—Don't jump in with a solution. It is usually much better if the other person comes up with the solution himself, even if it isn't the one you might have thought of! Ask a second, third, and fourth question to find out why he thinks and feels the way he does.
- *Ask about feelings*—Most people are much more comfortable with "the facts" than they are with discussing their emotions about those facts. Talking about feelings, however, often opens the door to real insight about the person. "How did you feel when that happened?" is a great question most of the time.
- *Ask about the conversation*—It can be quite revealing to ask someone how he feels about the conversation you are having with him right then. He may be glad you are interested, defensive that you are "so nosy," or confused because he hasn't usually been completely truthful before. Talking about your conversation may open the door to more honest communication in the future.

Another question to ask is, "What are you hearing me say?" That helps him reflect his observation so you can know if you have communicated clearly. It is also good to reflect back to him, "Let me tell you what I hear you saying."

We can all improve our listening skills so we better understand others and so those people feel that they are understood.

Principle #3: Love

If the root of codependency is the feeling of being unloved and not valued, you might expect a codependent to respond quickly and easily to love. This, however, usually isn't the case. The defense mechanisms that block pain and repress anger also stunt the person's ability to receive love. Or he may have learned not to trust another's love. Perhaps he has had people tell him they loved him who then condemned and neglected him.

Consistent words and acts of kindness may not seem to have much effect for a while, but they should slowly erode the person's defense mechanisms so that he actually *feels* loved. The love of God can be made real by *your* persistent, positive words and actions. Doctrine is important, but doctrine combined with a living model of the grace of God is far more powerful.

A friend of mine is feeling loved for the first time in his life. He recently told me, "I think I appreciate the kindness of others—especially my wife—more than anything else in the world. She has been loving and patient with me for years, but I didn't, or couldn't, feel it. Now her kindnesses mean so much to me!"

You think that everyone perceives love the same way you do. But they don't. You may also discover that some people rarely feel loved at all. Recently I was in a small group discussion when the conversation turned to this subject. I asked a woman how people communicate love to her. She replied, "When they tell me I've done a good job in my accounting work."

I had heard her discuss other aspects of her life in previous conversation, and I suspected that she seldom felt loved. I asked, "Do those comments make you feel loved, or do they make you feel appreciated for your performance?"

She looked at me with a confused, wondering stare. "I'm not sure I know the difference," she said finally.

People from dysfunctional families often have difficulty understanding and experiencing love. But another person's persistent compassion and honesty can pierce the hardness that has built up over the years so they can feel loved and valued.

Principle #4: Limits

Don't expect to make a codependent person healthy. You can't. There are limits to your responsibility in the relationship. But while you can't make him healthy, you *can* be loving and honest with him, and you can be healthy yourself. As long as he is willing to continue his healing process, you can continue to take steps with him. Yet when he consistently chooses to abdicate his responsibilities and reverts to his previous patterns of behavior, then it is time for you to reevaluate your responsibilities.

Jesus was supremely patient and kind to people. He spent long hours explaining and modeling the love of God to others. He loved them deeply, yet He never manipulated them. He warned people about the consequences of their decisions, but He always let them make their own choices.

Set limits. Learn to say no. Be honest. Don't allow the codependent person to control you with his self-pity or condemnation. But *talk* to him. Let him know *why* you are responding the way you are, and let him know the consequences of his behavior.

One young lady, Cheri, won people with her sweet disposition. She knew how to turn on the charm to get what she wanted and to get people to treat her the way she wanted to be treated. I have to admit that in our conversations I gave in to her a few times before I realized what was going on. First she asked me for a book because she didn't have enough money that day. Later she asked if we could change an appointment to a time that was inconvenient for me. I gave in. But when I became more objective, I began being honest with her and telling her no when I needed to.

The first time I was honest with her and didn't let her have her way, she cried and told me that I was treating her just like her mean father. I told her that I was not her father. I was simply making the choice I thought best so she would learn to be responsible for her own behavior. Then she got angry. When I didn't bend to that form of manipulation either, she was astounded. I told her how I felt about her behavior. I said, "I feel angry because you are trying to manipulate me to be responsible for you."

Cheri didn't come back to see me for several months, but she returned eventually. When she did, she knew I would be honest with her.

We can take someone through the healing process only as far as he or she is willing to go. It is his choice to take the next step. Our responsibility is to be honest, independent, and loving.

Now, let's turn from these general principles to some specific aspects of a primary role and a support role in the codependent's recovery process.

A Primary Role

A person who plays the primary role in the codependent's progress must be mature, stable, compassionate, perceptive, understanding of the issues, skillful in counseling, and must have time to devote to the relationship. That's a pretty tall order. But as we have seen, it is too easy to be manipulated and confused by the rescuing and control of a codependent. Below are some goals of a person in a primary role.

Provide a safe environment—A pastor, counselor, or mature friend in the primary role provides a safe haven for the codependent, who knows he can be honest and express what is really in his heart. The person in the primary role listens intently, draws out the other person, and helps him understand why he thinks, feels, and acts the way he does. The helper doesn't give simple answers and is patient during the long process of growth.

Demonstrate consistency—The codependent has lacked models of unconditional acceptance and strong support. His parents, sibling, or spouse may have withheld warmth or smothered him with too much control, which results in bonding and separateness problems. His perception of God probably reflects these distorted relationships, so he may view God as stern, harsh, condemning, aloof, or distant. As the caregiver consistently and patiently expresses love (especially when the codependent is hurting or angry and expects the helper to pull away or condemn), he establishes a model of the love and strength of God.

The person providing primary care must also be alert to the codependent's transference. When the helper discovers that he has taken the role of the hurtful important person in the rescuer's life, he should still remain constant in his love, honesty, and calmness.

Communicate love—In a loving environment, the codependent's defenses may come down so that he actually begins to feel loved and accepted. In fact, the counselor's demonstration of love may be a new experience, and the person may become quite attached to the counselor. He may even think the counselor is the most wonderful person who ever lived! That kind of attachment can be heady stuff, so it is important for the counselor to be stable, mature, and perceptive in order to help the codependent develop a number of solid, growing relationships. It is understandable for a hurting person to become extremely attached to the one by whom he feels loved and understood for the first time, but it is sad if the counselor doesn't direct him to other relationships so that a more healthy network can be developed.

Facilitate separateness—As the codependent learns to value himself in a loving environment, he will also learn to be separate in a positive way. He will come to value his own opinions without looking around to see if others agree with him every time. He will begin to feel what he really feels and want what he really wants. Such honesty is not narcissistic in the context of healthy, godly relationships. Rather it will lead to reality—the healthy experience of freedom in Christ, the desire to please Him, honesty about the tension between his old and new nature, and the understanding that all is not black or white.

The person playing the primary role can help the rescuer see when and how he rescues, which will help him choose to stop. He can help the codependent see when and how he controls others, so he will let them begin to make their own choices. And as the codependent is taught to value himself and be honest about life, he will no longer need to hide in denial and please people all the time.

I can personally attest to the importance of having a trustworthy person in the primary role of the healing process. A good friend filled this role in my life. He is the ultimate "safe" person. He is patient, consistent, a good listener, and he asks great questions. I feel like I can be myself when I'm with him, and the Lord has used him to touch areas of my life that I didn't even know existed. When these areas were first revealed, they hurt—a lot! But in the loving and strong environment my friend provided, I have been experiencing genuine healing in my life.

A Support Role

If your relationship with the codependent person has been strained because of your own needs as well as his, then you probably need to focus primarily on *your* needs first and play a support role in *his* life. The relational patterns that you and he have developed—fixing, withdrawing, denial, attacking, manipulating, etc.—prevent you from being an effective primary person to help him. Does that mean that you have forfeited any significant influence? No, not at all. Your own honesty, growth, and changes can have a tremendously powerful impact on him.

The wife of a man who is a controlling rescuer tried for years to help her husband. He was unresponsive, and worse, he resented his wife's insinuations that he had problems. But as she began learning about her own needs, her relationship with her husband changed. Instead of focusing only on *his* needs, she saw that *she* needed help. She told him, "I've been trying to get you to change, but *I* need to change, too. Recently, I've seen a lot of hurt in my relationship with my parents that I never knew was there. I've tried to fix your problems, but I've not been honest with you about my own problems. I'm sorry. Please forgive me. I want to change. I want to value you, your opinions, your feelings, and your choices."

Hers were not empty words. Over the course of the next several months she felt more pain, but she also experienced some real healing. As her husband saw her progress, his hard heart slowly melted and he began the healing process himself. As she related this story to me years later, she referred to this Scripture:

Why do you look at the speck that is in your brother's eye, but do not notice the log that is in your own eye? Or how can you say to your brother, 'Let me take the speck out of your eye,' and behold, the log is in your own eye? You hypocrite, first take the log out of your own eye, and then you will see clearly to take the speck out of your brother's eye.

Matthew 7:3-5

She told me, "I had to get the log out of my own eye first, and as I did, the Lord worked in my husband's life to accomplish far more than I ever dreamed!"

Some important instructions for someone in a support role include:

- Be honest about your own needs, feelings, and desires.
- Be an active listener.
- Affirm the codependent in his strengths.
- Affirm the person as he takes steps in the healing process.
- Be genuine in your praise. Phony praise is counterproductive.
- Don't give much advice.
- Let the person make his own decisions.
- Don't try to make the codependent feel good and get healthy quickly. (Don't fix him!)
- Let the person have his opinions *without* commenting on them.

Most of us are quick to give our "valuable" analysis of others' opinions. We're only trying to help, aren't we? We say, "Yes, but..." or "Have you thought about...?" or "If I were in your shoes, I'd...." Even when we see things in his ideas that we could improve, it is much more important for him to feel valued than to get our input so he can be exactly right. Our opinions are not indispensable. Our affirmation is much more important to hurting people than our advice.

If we have a history of manipulating and condemning the codependent, our advice won't be welcome at all. It will be seen as manipulation—even if we are well-meaning in our motives.

Scott was unwilling to listen to any suggestions his mother made because he felt so hurt by her. Until she earns his trust by consistently affirming him and encouraging his separateness, she would be wise to avoid giving any more advice.

A support role can be very influential in the rescuer's life. Hopefully, he will find someone to be the primary caregiver sooner or later so he will make better progress. If his progress takes an extended time and your own progress continues strongly, you can have even more influence in helping him develop perception and experience love and separateness. Whether you play a support role or a primary role in a codependent's life, you can have a profound influence during his healing process.

Summary

1. In what ways are you a good listener?

2. How could you become a better listener?

3. What kind of role (support or primary) do you *want* to play in your friend's or relative's life? Why?

4. What kind of role (support or primary) *should* you play in your friend's or relative's life? Why?

5. What can you do to help the other person make progress? Be specific.

6. What errors do you need to avoid as you assume your role?

Endnotes

[1] *"Transference* occurs during psychoanalysis when the patient attributes to the therapist feelings, reactions, animosities, and affections that he now holds or has held toward important people in his life. Freud considered this an irrational, but highly significant, part of psychotherapy. In fact, the therapist structures the situation in a way that almost assures the occurrence of such a relationship: the professional and social distance that he maintains; his positioning behind the patient during therapy; his interpretation of the patient's seemingly most inconsequential remarks and actions—all contribute to the transference. In a sense the therapist becomes an inkblot toward which the patient reacts, albeit unconsciously, as he did vis-á-vis important figures in his life. For example, the therapist may be perceived as the patient's mother, spouse, or sibling, sometimes even becoming the recipient of the same love or hate that the patient held for them.

The development and resolution of the transference is a major part of psychoanalysis because the patient-to-therapist relationship is primarily a product of the patient's imagination and therefore provides the therapist with invaluable information about the patient's basic conflicts and infantile responses. It also affords opportunities to help the patient gain awareness of these reactions so he or she will learn to discriminate between old conflicts and the new ones directed toward the therapist. The best way to facilitate such discrimination is to react neutrally, and hence differently, from early figures in the patient's life.

But transference can also create difficulties during psychoanalysis. The therapist must guard against reciprocating the patient's feelings by 'acting-out' with his or her own *counter-transference*, or emotional reactions. This requires that the psychoanalyst have a thorough understanding of his or her own motivations and personality."

Benjamin Kleinmuntz, *Essentials of Abnormal Psychology*, 2nd ed., (San Francisco: Harper and Row, 1980), pp. 482-483.

² Adapted from *Team Building Seminar,* Minneapolis, MN: Campus Crusade for Christ, 1987, pp. 42-44.

Section 3

Facilitating the Healing Process in the Codependent's Life

The process of healing for the codependent in your life includes both behaviors and identity, both thought patterns and feelings, both his relationship with God and his relationships with others. Like climbing a mountain, the process is usually long and slow with lots of starts and stops. But with encouragement and patience, real progress can be made.

Chapter 10

The Codependent Needs . . . Perception

Several years ago I had the opportunity to go to Thailand. On the plane, our group had a crash course on the Thai culture. (For example, it is extremely offensive to show the sole of your foot to anyone, so you shouldn't cross your legs.) We talked about greetings, etiquette, uniqueness of the people and the religion, and we talked about the kinds of food the Thai people might serve us. We thought we were prepared.

One night our group was taken to a special banquet. We sat outside on grass mats and saw a local band and dancers. Then our first course was served. "What is that?" I whispered to a friend.

"I don't know, but I'm not sure I'm going to eat it," was the reply. Yet we decided to take the risk, and sure enough, we didn't die.

After a while, the main course arrived. I looked at it. It looked at me. I watched everybody else, especially our smiling host, to see what to do. I pondered the idea of taking a cab somewhere, but I didn't even know where I was, much less where I would go. Besides, my Thai language skills were a bit rusty. (And I was still trying to figure out how to sit on the ground for long periods of time without showing the soles of my feet!)

After carefully analyzing the intended victim (the one on the plate), I realized that other people were tenuously dissecting and masticating their beasts. I prayed. I took a bite. And I thought, *Hey, it's not bad!*

We have been studying the land and culture of codependents. We have reflected on how we relate to them and how our own idiosyncrasies and needs affect our relationships with them. Now it's time to learn to relate in new ways.

Whenever we relate to people in other cultures, often *we* are the ones who learn the most. That may happen as we learn to relate to the codependents in our lives.

Perception, love, and separateness. These three characteristics provide handles for the needs of codependents. The three are inextricably linked as they build on one another and are dependent on each other. Here, and in the next two chapters, we will look at each characteristic separately, but we will see the interconnections. We will also see how perception, love, and separateness relate to each of the characteristics of codependency.

The perception that we are describing in this chapter is an accurate perception of reality. It is truth. This kind of perception seems to be tremendously important to God. Even the most random sampling of the Scriptures shows how the Lord has consistently sent messengers to mankind to provide a clear perception of His character and our needs. Noah spoke of the righteousness of God and called people to repent of their wickedness (Genesis 6—7; 2 Peter 2:5). Moses was privileged to be in the very presence of God and to communicate His name to the Israelites as he led them out of Egyptian slavery. Isaiah communicated both comfort and judgment to God's people. David's adultery with Bathsheba and murder of Uriah prompted God to send Nathan to confront David. After realizing that God doesn't want people to hide their sins and needs, David wrote:

> *Behold, Thou dost desire truth in the innermost being, and in the hidden part Thou wilt make me know wisdom.*
>
> Psalms 51:6

Jesus proclaimed the importance of perception when He spoke to the multitudes on the mountain:

> *The lamp of the body is the eye; if therefore your eye is clear, your whole body will be full of light.*
>
> *But if your eye is bad, your whole body will be full of darkness. If therefore the light that is in you is darkness, how great is the darkness!*
>
> Matthew 6:22-23

The Apostle Paul twice instructed believers to "speak truth" and to speak it "in love" to one another (Ephesians 4:15, 25). He also recognized that we need to be honest about the individual needs of people around us:

> We urge you, brethren, admonish the unruly, encourage the fainthearted, help the weak, be patient with all men.
>
> 1 Thessalonians 5:14

The beauty and grandeur of nature itself gives us a perception of God's glory (Psalms 19:1-6), and His law gives us more specific insight into His character (Psalms 19:7-14). The Holy Spirit communicates truth and gives perception to receptive hearts about sin, righteousness, and judgment (John 16:7-15). Many other passages (including Hebrews 1, Philippians 2, and John 1) record the fact that Jesus Christ was revealed to man to demonstrate the love, power, and glory of God.

The primary responsibility of teaching and developing perception lies with the family (Deuteronomy 6:4-12; Proverbs 3:1-4). This brings us to the central point of this chapter. Dysfunctional families fail, to one degree or another in a couple of areas: either to impart truth accurately, or more importantly, to develop the mechanisms (belief systems) which enable family members to *perceive* accurately. When these mechanisms are damaged or undeveloped, truth becomes distorted. Adding more truth won't solve the problem until the underlying mechanisms are developed. The problem then, in dysfunctional families, is not just one of misinformation. The root problem is that the ability to accurately perceive is damaged. A codependent may have learned to "read" others very well (in order to please them), but he doesn't recognize reality in his own life or the motives for his interactions with others.

This is why more truth doesn't necessarily bring about healthy, positive, deep, lasting change in a codependent's life. Most of us know plenty of people (and many of us *are* those people) who have had good Bible teaching, gone to excellent seminars, read wonderful books, and have notebooks full of truth. Yet changes are superficial and fleeting. Oh, at times we may get really excited and believe we finally found some answers, but if we don't accurately perceive ourselves and the world around us, the changes don't last. Or if they *do* last, they become rigid systems (like the Pharisees had) which control outward behavior but don't bring inward healing, life, love, freedom, or hope.

Solomon instructed people to gain truth, but he also admonished them to develop perception mechanisms (discernment and wisdom) to enable them to recognize and apply that truth:

> *Hear, O sons, the instruction of a father, and give attention*
> *that you may gain understanding,*
> *For I give you sound teaching; do not abandon my instruction.*
> *When I was a son to my father, tender and the only son in the*
> *sight of my mother,*
> *Then he taught me and said to me, "Let your heart hold fast my*
> *words; keep my commandments and live;*
> *Acquire wisdom! Acquire understanding! Do not forget, nor turn*
> *away from the words of my mouth."*
>
> Proverbs 4:1-5

> *O naive ones, discern prudence; and, O fools, discern wisdom.*
>
> Proverbs 8:5

> *By wisdom a house is built, and by understanding it is established.*
>
> Proverbs 24:3

How, then, can a person from a dysfunctional family develop mechanisms for a more accurate perception of reality? It is difficult. But it *is* possible if he gets involved in relationships with honest, loving, perceptive, patient people. These people need to help him: (1) *Identify* codependent traits in his life, (2) *Detach* to understand them and to reflect on truth as he develops a mechanism of perception, and (3) *Decide* to take positive, productive steps toward health. Your particular part in this process will vary depending on whether you play a support or a primary role.

Help The Other Person Identify Distorted Perceptions

We can't *make* people see reality. We are only responsible to "speak the truth in love," not to force them to acknowledge that truth. Several years ago, I spent some time with a lady who had a reputation of being a leader, but there was an undercurrent of cynicism about her. Some believed she was a wonderful, charismatic, powerful influencer of others. Others thought she was a manipulative power-seeker. After a few hours with her in a group meeting, I could sense people's opinions about her polarizing in one of these two extremes.

After several more meetings, our group began to come apart at the seams! This lady's attentiveness and warmth had won quite a loyal following from most of the people, but several others resented her growing influence. Later I asked her about the differing views toward her. She retorted, "They're just jealous. I'm only trying to build up people. Didn't Jesus do the same thing? They just don't know how to affirm people." Then with obvious disgust she added, "Nobody understands me. I build good relationships. God uses me in people's lives, and others resent it!"

I tried to talk to her about the way she came across in meetings. (She created a commanding silence as people waited for clues as to what *she* was thinking.) I also made some suggestions about how she could develop more unity in the group. But she walked away from me. I could tell I was now firmly entrenched on the "enemy" side of her ledger.

A few days later, another of the group members (one who had resented the blind loyalty of her fawning following) confronted her. Again she sat in disgusted silence, hearing but not listening.

Several others confronted her about her control of the group by "serving and loving," but it seemed that her ears were closed to anyone who disagreed with her in the least. Her perception was distorted and there was nothing any of us could do to change it.

I have known other people who staunchly refused to listen, even when confronted lovingly by several people over the course of months or years. Fortunately, most of them eventually began to respond.

Gary is a Christian from a workaholic home who had believed that counseling was one step this side of the Lake of Fire. He had told others that to solve problems, "All we need is the Bible." Gary spent several months developing a friendship with another believer, Dan, who is more realistic about life. And slowly—very slowly—Gary began to listen as Dan related his own struggles, hopes, and fears. The automatic defenses in Gary's heart began to take a little longer before cutting Dan off, and finally Gary began to see that he had a few problems to deal with, too. There was a crack in the door.

The first important aspect of helping someone identify faulty perception is to be honest about your own struggles with perception. Also, seeing truth and deception in print is a valuable help for them. One of the best tools I have ever seen to help do this is Robert S. McGee's book and workbook, *The Search for Significance* (Rapha Publishing/Word, Inc.). Consistently over the years, I have seen "the lights come on" in people's hearts as they have reflected on the questions in the workbook. This chart gives a synopsis of the material.

FALSE BELIEFS	CONSEQUENCES OF FALSE BELIEFS	GOD'S SPECIFIC SOLUTION	RESULTS OF GOD'S SOLUTION
I must meet certain standards in order to feel good about myself.	The fear of failure; perfectionism; being driven to succeed; manipulating others to achieve success; withdrawing from healthy risks	*Because of justification, I am completely forgiven and fully pleasing to God. I no longer have to fear failure.*	Increasing freedom from the fear of failure; desire to pursue the right things: Christ and His kingdom; love for Christ
I must have the approval of certain others to feel good about myself.	The fear of rejection; attempting to please others at any cost; being overly sensitive to criticism; withdrawing from others to avoid disapproval	*Because of reconciliation, I am totally accepted by God. I no longer have to fear rejection.*	Increasing freedom from the fear of rejection; willingness to be open and vulnerable; able to relax around others; willingness to take criticism; desire to please God no matter what others think
Those who fail (including myself) are unworthy of love and deserve to be punished.	The fear of punishment; propensity to punish others; blaming self and others for personal failure; withdrawing from God and fellow believers; being driven to avoid punishment	*Because of propitiation, I am deeply loved by God. I no longer have to fear punishment or punish others.*	Increasing freedom from the fear of punishment; patience and kindness toward others; being quick to apply forgiveness; deep love for Christ
I am what I am. I cannot change. I am hopeless.	Feelings of shame, hopelessness, inferiority; passivity; loss of creativity; isolation, withdrawing from others	*Because of regeneration, I have been made brand new, complete in Christ. I no longer need to experience the pain of shame.*	Christ-centered self-confidence; joy, courage, peace; desire to know Christ

Many of the negative assumptions which plague codependents (and others) are addressed in *The Search for Significance:*

- the compulsion to please people in order to avoid rejection
- the drive to succeed in order to win others' approval or meet our own arbitrary standards
- the feeling that we have to be perfect, coupled with intense guilt because we aren't
- the fear of condemnation because of our sins or failures
- the morbid analysis of what we say, think, feel, or do that leads to feelings of intense shame about ourselves
- the feelings of loneliness while wearing a facade of friendliness
- the attempts to control others through praise or condemnation

My previous book, *Codependency,* also has a chart which summarizes the codependent's thoughts, feelings, and actions (which were introduced in Chapter 6, page 111). A look at these characteristics may help a codependent begin to identify problem issues in his life.

Don't dump all this information on the other person at once! Be patient. Be selective. And be honest about your own growing perceptions. Only then may he slowly begin to see some of the reality in his life.

Help Him Detach

As the other person *identifies* misperceptions, he learns to see reality. *Detaching* involves trying to understand the source of his newfound reality and learning how to proceed from this point. At first, most of us see only a few symptoms of our problems. But as we detach and reflect with someone who is understanding and compassionate, we begin to see the causes of the problems.

Sometimes it is very difficult to ascertain the cause of pain, anger, and denial because we have received so many "mixed messages" from our families. A young lady recently described her family to me. She was confused. She was beginning to feel a lot of hurt, but she felt guilty for feeling it.

"How did you feel while you were growing up in your home?" I asked.

"I felt guilty a lot. I tried my best...made good grades and everything. I wanted my parents to be proud of me, and they were—most of the time. When I went away to college, though, they got really upset with me."

"So...you felt like you had to do everything just right?"

"Yes, but I always knew my parents loved me completely. I've never had a problem with that. My mother has always devoted her life to make me happy," she said confidently. "I don't know why I'm so insecure and feel so guilty. I guess there's something really wrong with me."

After more conversation, I said to her, "It seems that you received mixed messages from your folks. They *said* they loved you, yet that love was based on you doing exactly what they wanted. Could it be that they didn't respect you enough to let you make your own decisions and live your own life?"

She looked puzzled at first, but soon saw what I meant. "So that's why I've felt so bad even though they said they loved me," she said quietly.

Mixed messages are particularly deceptive. People tend to cling to the positive statements on the surface, but they internalize the underlying negative messages while refusing to admit that they even exist. As my wife, Joyce, accurately observed, "Mixed messages will make you crazy!"

As you help a codependent detach and reflect, be aware of two very significant issues: the character of God and forgiveness. If one's perception of God comes from his relationship with his parents, then someone from a dysfunctional family probably has a distorted view of God. (Of course, no one of us has an absolutely accurate view of God, but people from dysfunctional families usually have a more distorted perception.)

Take time to talk about the other person's concept of God and forgiveness. You will probably find that he can articulate theological truth, but further reflection may reveal that superficial responses hide deeper feelings that God is harsh or distant, and that forgiveness is based on his ability to appease God by doing good things or feeling sorry enough long enough. The model you set of the love and forgiveness of God added to your honest discussion of distortions and truth can be a powerful combination for positive change.

Many codependent Christians have the simplistic view that "obedience produces happiness." They explain that their problems stem from neglecting certain activities such as Bible reading, church attendance, or prayer. They are driven to "do the right things," and they expect to feel better for doing them. They may, indeed, feel better for a while, but "doing" is only part of life. "Being" is the foundation for doing and gives meaning to the things we do. "Being" focuses on who we are, not what we do. For Christians, it is based solidly on our identity in Christ.

We are loved, forgiven, accepted, complete, declared righteous, and destined to spend eternity with the Lord. We are God's beloved children—not because we earned the privilege but because it was freely given to us. God, then, is our Provider and Protector. He is the One who has committed Himself to our welfare. Yet "doing" is easier to monitor than "being" because comprehending our identity in Christ takes time, honesty, and deep relationships. Such requirements can be too threatening for a hurting person who wants quick results.

Even when someone enters the process and starts to develop an accurate perception, he can have unrealistic expectations about the time it will take to change. He understands the need for a process, but he wants it to be over today! A good friend of mine started going through this process, and I told her to be patient and look for changes over months and years, not days. A few weeks later, she called to tell me, "I hate the word *process*!" Yet her persistence is paying off. She is doing extremely well at this point, partially because she has a more realistic appraisal of the time her process will take.

Perception comes in spurts and stages. And as the person detaches, he is tempted to think that each new insight is the greatest and deepest he will ever have. Well, it is—for now. God is very gracious to take us by the hand and lead us slowly, one step at a time. Each new insight usually has enough pain to deal with on its own. I'm glad God doesn't give us more than that or we would be overwhelmed.

Help the codependent person detach by patiently discussing the issues in this chapter. The following questions may help in your discussion:

- Why do you think he said/did that to you?
- What did he mean?
- How do you feel about it?

- How would a healthy person feel?
- Is he controlling you? Condemning you? Neglecting you?
- Why do you feel guilty? Driven? Afraid? Lonely?
- Are you rescuing?
- Are you acting as a savior? A Judas?

These statements also may help him develop convictions:

- You aren't responsible for making him happy.
- You aren't responsible for fixing the problem.
- He needs to be responsible for himself.
- You can respond calmly.
- You can say no.
- You can say yes.
- You can make your own decisions.
- You feel angry...lonely...guilty...driven...afraid.
- You are loved, forgiven, and accepted by God through Jesus Christ.
- What are realistic expectations? How does he usually respond to you?
- What do you want from this conversation (or visit, encounter, etc.)?
- What if you do this:_____?
- How can you respond if this happens?

These questions and statements can become the basis for a lot of good discussion. Then the person needs to decide on the best course of action.

Help The Other Person Decide

Remember that one of a codependent's frequent, major problems is that he expects others to make decisions for him. Your role at this point may be to make suggestions or ask questions like, "What do you think you ought to do?" If he asks for your advice, be careful that he doesn't do what you suggest simply because he wants your approval. It may be wise to discuss with him the limits of your role and your desire for him to make his own decisions.

Some people make decisions impulsively, not taking time or energy to reflect on the consequences. Others get bogged down by fears of terrible unseen consequences. The first kind of person needs help in reflecting; the second needs help in detaching (and feeling more affirmed and confident take the next step). Both require much perception and patience on your part.

Decisions can be grouped into three categories: reading, relationships, and risks.

Reading—One decision the codependent needs to make is to learn as much as he can about codependency. It is helpful if he writes down his observations and questions. Reading, reflecting, and writing usually help the person internalize truth and recognize distortions more easily. You can help by suggesting resources and discussing codependency issues with him in order to help him process the information.

Relationships—Another decision the codependent can make is to take specific steps to develop healthy relationships. You can invite him to evaluate his current relationships and encourage him to pursue more healthy ones. You might suggest that he get involved with a group of people who are learning and growing in this same area. You can ask him some of the following questions: Who are some people who are learning and growing in their perceptions? Where can you find such people? How can you get through the first awkward stages in developing these relationships?

Risks—As the codependent develops a more accurate perception, he will discover aspects of relationships which need to be corrected. His attempts to change these relationships can be risky. Many people, especially family members, will resist change and try to force him back into his usual role. You can offer much encouragement for him to take those risks, but don't force him to. He must learn to make his own decisions.

Risk is a natural part of life for most healthy people. Setting limits is a risky proposition. Telling someone the truth is frightening, especially if it is a family member. But taking these risks usually yields much more insight. The more a codependent is willing to risk, the better his prospects are for genuine healing.

One man told me how he took the step of being honest with his father about the father's condemnation over the years. He exclaimed, "My palms were sweating and my voice quaked. I had to have everything written out so I wouldn't go blank. But I did it! I learned so much about how my Dad has affected me. It has really hurt, but it's given me a lot more insight. Now I see it all!"

"Well," I encouraged him, "that's terrific!" (I didn't want to dampen his enthusiasm by telling him that although he had seen a significant part of the reality of his relationship with his father, he still hadn't yet "seen it all.")

Perception is the foundation for the other two characteristic needs of codependents: love and separateness. As you help the codependent gain insight into his struggle and undertake the process of overcoming these struggles, every aspect of his life will be positively affected.

Summary

Think of the codependent in your life. Then look over this chapter again and write out a plan to help him identify, detach, and decide as he develops perception.

How to Help Him Identify:

How to Help Him Detach:

How to Help Him Decide:

Discuss this plan with your friend or relative. Make compromises and
modifications so that you are both satisfied with it. And then, by all means,
encourage him to risk taking the first steps that are required for him to begin the
long (but rewarding) process of healing.

Chapter 11

The Codependent Needs . . . Love

Walt is a friend of mine in the insurance business. About two years ago, Walt started to recognize a compulsion to be a caretaker and rescuer. Recently, we had lunch together and he wanted to tell me about all he has been learning. He explained, "I've been a driven man all my life: driven to succeed in my business, driven to make money, and driven to have a nice house. I felt like I had to make everybody happy: my parents, my wife, my children, my boss—my dog! Everybody! Now I look back on all that. I lived with a constant, high level of tension in my life. I guess I was afraid somebody would find out who I *really* am...afraid somebody wouldn't like my work, that they might not respect me. So I did all I could for everybody I could."

"In the last couple of years, I've seen that a lot of my drivenness has been an effort to win love. I won some respect and had a few laughs, but I still didn't really feel loved. I had a lot of anger built up, and when I got honest about it, well, it wasn't pretty! But now I'm starting to learn about love—real love." Tears came to Walt's eyes. "I don't think I've ever known what love was before."

Walt's father and mother were divorced when he was four years old, and his mother had never achieved emotional stability after that. In the midst of her needs, Walt had learned to rescue her. Having grown up in a dysfunctional family, Walt was unable to experience and express love.

Some professionals estimate that 96% of families are dysfunctional to some degree. In these families, the ability to receive and give love is not adequately developed. Even when love *is* expressed to a family member, it isn't received and felt. In Walt's case, his wife had genuinely loved him for years, but he had great difficulty in sensing her affection. It was as if his receptors for receiving and transmitting love were damaged and inoperable.

These broken receptors are illustrated poignantly in the example of Laura, a six-year-old girl. Her parents came to me explaining that Laura was having problems. She wasn't rebellious, yet she was unresponsive to them. Her father was an angry man who, it appeared, seldom communicated warmth and tenderness to Laura. He explained, "The other day I told Laura to come give me a hug, but she didn't move. I walked over to hug her, but when I did, her arms hung down at her sides. I asked her why she didn't hug me back, and she said, 'I don't have any arms.'"

Laura's receptors had been damaged by her angry father so that even when he did communicate love, she couldn't receive it or express it back to him.

This chapter is about the codependent's need to experience and express love. Yet we will spend most of the time focusing on pain because repressed pain and broken receptors are realities which cannot be sidestepped. In fact, as the hurting codependent is encouraged to be honest about his life, the door is opened for real relationships. In spite of the hurt and anger he begins to feel, he also discovers that some people won't give up on him just because he isn't perfect. He will begin to sense that somebody cares.

As the person experiences the new sensation of people asking caring questions instead of demanding his instant rescuing, he will begin to feel valued as a person. As he takes the risk of being honest about his weaknesses and sins, he can experience the forgiveness and acceptance of others (especially yours). As people listen to him without correcting him, he will gain confidence. As others let him make his own decisions, feel his own feelings, and think his own thoughts, he will gain a new sense of strength. As people genuinely care for him, he will learn to experience authentic love. He will begin to believe that God isn't as harsh or aloof as he originally thought. He will begin to genuinely experience the tender, strong, consistent love of God for him. And he will then learn to express that love to others.

God has gone to the greatest lengths to communicate His love to us and show us how important it is to love one another. The covenants in the Old Testament spoke of the relationship He wants with us. He communicated His lovingkindness which proved that He was, and is, committed to loving His people. The prophets repeatedly admonished wayward people to return to God, who is both just and forgiving. The incarnation and the crucifixion occurred because "God so loved the world." Our relationship with God is one of warmth and intimacy (Romans 8:15). Nothing can separate us from His perfect love, His affection and good will, or His unconditional acceptance (Romans 8:35-39). And our eternity will be spent attempting to plumb the depths of His love. Paul wrote the believers in Ephesus:

> *God, being rich in mercy, because of His great love with which He loved us...raised us up with Him, and seated us with Him in the heavenly places, in Christ Jesus, in order that in the ages to come He might show the surpassing riches of His grace in kindness toward us in Christ Jesus.*
>
> Ephesians 2:4, 6-7

As we experience the unfathomable love of God (Ephesians 3:19), our character and our Christian growth will reflect His love (Galatians 5:22-23; 2 Peter 1:5-7). Our relationships, too, will be chiefly characterized by compassion, love, forgiveness, and kindness (1 Corinthians 13; John 13:34-35; Ephesians 4:31-32; Romans 12:9-21; et al).

The change brought about by the love of God was powerfully shown in the film *Jesus*. To me, the most penetrating scene was the depiction of the sinful woman who entered the threatening inner sanctions of a Pharisee's house where Jesus and the disciples were dining. Somehow, she had sensed Jesus love, forgiveness, and acceptance of her, and she was bold in expressing her deep appreciation. Luke describes the scene:

> *She brought an alabaster vial of perfume, and standing behind Him at His feet, weeping, she began to wet His feet with her tears, and kept wiping them with the hair of her head, and kissing His feet, and anointing them with the perfume.*
>
> Luke 7:37-38

The self-righteous Pharisee did not even give Christ the customary greeting, much less display such elaborate affection. But the woman had felt a deep need for love and forgiveness, and had experienced them in an overflowing measure. The person who had not sensed his need didn't experience or express love in his relationship with Christ.

How do receptors get damaged? Why do codependents talk so much about love and experience it so little? How can receptors be repaired so that they can, like this woman in Luke's Gospel, genuinely experience and express love? Let's examine these issues.

Help The Other Person Identify the Extent to Which He Hasn't Experienced Unconditional Love

If authentic love hasn't been experienced or expressed to a great degree in a codependent's life, what *has* he experienced? Many people from dysfunctional families, including codependents, don't really know how they feel. The instability of the family creates a situation that is very threatening. People are out of control. They may explode in anger. They may be depressed. They may feel everything intensely. They may be numb. The subconscious assumption is that people who are out of control need to somehow be controlled. The easiest way is to deny one's own hurt and anger—and hope everybody else does, too. So people learn not to be honest about painful emotions. They learn to clamp them and not let them come to the surface.

After years of repression, many are completely unaware of the hurt and anger inside them. One young woman was abused as a child, but she told me, "I wasn't really affected. I don't feel angry at all." A man explained, "It's amazing that my father's alcoholism and my mother's other boyfriends didn't bother me emotionally!" It often takes weeks of in-depth discussions to uncover real emotions. The time required depends on a number of factors: the environment, the skills of the friend or counselor, the warmth communicated, the strength of the codependent's defense mechanisms, etc. Sooner or later, however, the uncovered emotions include hurt, bitterness, emptiness, fear, loneliness, and an assortment of related pains.

Women seem to more readily admit hurt or fear in their lives. Anger may make them appear too threatening or out of control. Men, on the other hand, often identify anger more readily because expressing anger seems more socially acceptable than showing hurt or fear. Eventually, however, both men and women usually admit to hurt, fear, *and* anger.

People in dysfunctional families often communicate mixed messages. They *say* they love each other, but tones of voice, gestures, and expressions often communicate disgust or condemnation rather than genuine love. The mind may register, "They love me," but the heart says, "No they don't." Children in these families want to believe that their parents are stable, loving, secure, and right. So whenever there's something wrong, they assume, *There is something wrong with me!* Objectivity may be threatening, but denial and self-denigration are terribly destructive for the child—and for the adult who used to be that child.

As you help a codependent identify the hurt, fear, anger, or other repressed emotions in his life, be patient. Defenses from years of repression don't fall away easily. As the other person gets in touch with the fears, hurts, and anger from his past, he can experience the deep healing of God's love and the love of those who genuinely value him. This process isn't simple. It is often long and painful, but through it, a person can rebuild damaged receptors and learn to give and receive real love.

Consider asking questions like the ones below. And as the other person responds, be sure to ask many follow-up questions. And listen!

- How did your parents relate to each other when you were young?
- How did you relate to your brothers or sisters?
- How did your mother relate to you?
- How did your father relate to you?
- What are the happiest moments of your childhood? What happened? How did you feel?
- What are your saddest or scariest childhood memories? What happened? How did you feel?
- Describe some other important relationships. How did those affect you?
- How do you think you've been positively affected by your parents, siblings, others? Negatively?
- How would you define and describe *love*?

Writing is an exercise which might help your friend or relative get more in touch with repressed emotions. After you have asked him the questions listed above, consider having him write a letter to each person who has deeply affected him. Assure him that he doesn't need to send the letters! Putting his thoughts on paper is just for his benefit. He may need some help getting started. Have him try something like:

> *Dear Mother,*
> *Something I wish had been true in my childhood is...*
> *Sometimes I felt...*
> *I wish you would have...*

Be sure to discuss these with your friend or relative after the letters have been written. A lot of repressed emotions could come out! A lot of healing can begin!

Note: *Your Parents and You* (Rapha Publishing/Word, Inc.) is a book which contains information to help a person understand the benefits and liabilities of his family.

Help Him Detach

Love is a major requirement for the process of emotional healing, as well as the product of it. As you communicate loving compassion and affirmation, your codependent relative or friend can find the courage to be open and honest. He is probably afraid you will go away if he doesn't act "just right," gets angry, cries, or doesn't say what he thinks you want him to say. At some point, he will probably test your relationship to see if you really care.

Your honesty about your own life and consistent affirmation of him will build trust. Genuine progress usually follows after trust is established.

As you help him detach to reflect on why he feels hurt, afraid, or angry, it is important to help him see that he is both a victim and a victimizer. He is the victim of others' neglect, abuse, or manipulation, but he probably treats others in similarly harmful ways. As a victimizer, he may not mirror the same ways he has been treated. He may treat others in different, but equally destructive, manners. For example:

- If he has been smothered and rescued, he may smother and rescue others or he may withdraw and be passive.
- If he was abused, he may abuse others or he may rescue them.
- If he has been neglected, he may be neglectful or he may rescue or abuse others.

In any of these situations, a harmful relational pattern is perpetuated.

Whether giving or receiving, codependents tend to confuse love with forms of control. The word *love* may be misused to describe any of these traits. As you discuss the other person's behavior with him and he uses certain terms, keep asking, "How do you *experience* these?" and "How do you *express* these?" Keep in mind that rescuers tend to confuse a lot of different things with genuine love. Rescuers tend to...

Confuse pity with love—Their "loving" statements are often: "I'm so sorry for you. I wish that hadn't happened. That's just awful. You poor thing."

When you fail in some way, the codependent expresses a "black" perspective: "What a tragedy!"

Confuse worry with love—This is a bit more aggressive than pity: "I have been *so* worried about you! I didn't know what in the world would happen to you! You really need to take care of yourself better! I've been up *all night* worrying about you!"

When you fail in some way, the codependent may say, "I just *knew* it!"

Confuse domination with love—"I know what's best for you. I am 45 years old, and I have handled that situation many times before. You'd better do it like I tell you or you'll be sorry! After all, nobody loves you like I do, and nobody knows what's best for you better than I do."

When you fail in some way, he retorts, "You should have listened to me!"

Confuse need with love—"I need you *so much*. You don't know how much you help me. You're the *only one* who really understands me and cares about me!"

When you fail in some way, the codependent responds with either denial: "Oh, it doesn't matter"; or condemnation: "You let me down!"

Confuse rescuing with love—"I'll be glad to help you Here, let me do that for you. It doesn't matter. I don't mind working so hard for you. Boy, you need help! You're lucky I came along!"

When you fail in some way, he responds with either more rescuing: "That's okay, I'll fix it," or condemnation: "I can't believe it. You let me down when I needed you!"

Confuse correction with love—"Get your arm off the table! Don't forget your wallet. Be sure to remember... You'd better... Don't..."

When you fail in some way, he communicates condemnation, "I can't believe it! You did it again!"

In dysfunctional families, virtually all a person does is an attempt to win love because he wants it so much. His deep longing for love and the lack of fulfillment leads him to confuse love with these poor substitutes, all of which can be intensely controlling. Some are subtle. Some are sledgehammers. Obviously they are not all wrong all of the time. Everyone needs occasional helpful advice and compassion. The test of whether another's advice is helpful or harmful depends on the tone and frequency of those communications. A good rule of thumb is that twenty positive communications counterbalance one negative one. We need to communicate more than a 20 to 1 ratio of affirmation, trust and love to remain on the positive side of the scale.

As we have seen in dysfunctional families, many of the seemingly positive communications are actually manipulative, so they can't be included on the positive side of the ledger. This observation is not meant to belittle or condemn. It is designed to give us understanding. Those who communicate using condemnation, manipulation, or neglect have deep hurts themselves. They need our objectivity and compassion, not reciprocal condemnation.

As you help the codependent in your life detach and reflect, discuss both the hurts and the joys of life. Many people are overwhelmed with the deep pain, anger, emptiness, or loneliness which can surface at various points during their progress. The stark reality of intense anger or painful rejection can be a scary thing—both for him and for you. But don't provide simplistic answers. Love the other person.

Affirm him. Be there for him. As his hurts are exposed and expressed, he can experience genuine healing and hope. He can feel loved.

Help The Other Person Decide

Again, it is important that you not rescue a codependent person by making his decisions for him. He needs to develop the skills and the confidence so he can make decisions on his own. It may be painful to watch him struggle with decisions, but that is a part of the process. Be sure to explain why you aren't making his decisions so that he won't think you are withdrawing love from him. Clearly understand your role—support or primary—so that you will have a very positive impact in this vital area of his development. Encourage him to read, to be involved in healthy relationships and to take risks to give and receive love.

Reading—Articles, tapes, and books which describe the distorted working of dysfunctional families and the road to health will garrison the other person's mind with clearer perceptions of healthy and unhealthy patterns of relationships. Also, there are some wonderful books about the love of God and how we can experience and express it, such as *Jesus Loves Me* (Roush, Belpre, Ohio) or *The Four Loves* (Harcourt Brace Jovanovich, Inc.).

Relationships—No matter how much a person reads and studies about loving relationships, nothing takes the place of being involved in one (or two). We all need to feel that somebody cares so we will believe we have some value. Developing relationships takes time, attention, and real love.

Jan's husband just got out of the drug rehab program at a local hospital. She dreaded his coming home. She said in an exasperated voice, "He's coming home, and he'll expect me to take care of him again. I can't do it. I just can't do it. I can't give anymore. I'm a dry well."

Jan was directed to a group of people who are struggling, but progressing through their codependency. "For the first time in years," she told me, "I feel like somebody understands how I feel. Somebody cares!" Those supportive relationships have provided strength and encouragement for Jan not only to survive her marriage, but really grow.

Risks—Risks are always a part of love: the risk of being known, the risk of rejection, the risk of feeling things that are new, the risk of many unknowns. Jan took those risks. Even though she was desperate, she wanted to hang up as she made that first call to the group leader. As she drove to the meeting, she wanted to drive back home. As she walked to the door, she wanted to run away. But she didn't. "I didn't have much courage," she said, "but I had just enough!"

Summary

You can't make your friend or relative read a book about his problems. You can't make him get involved in relationships. You can't make him take risks that he doesn't want to take. But you *can* be honest. You can care. You can affirm him. And when it's needed, you can calmly tell him the consequences of not taking the next step in developing open, honest relationships with people who genuinely care about him. That's how Jesus treated people, and it's a model we need to learn to follow.

Look over the chapter again and write out a plan to help the codependent person in your life identify, detach, and decide as he learns to experience and express love.

How to Help Him Identify:

How to Help Him Detach:

How to Help Him Decide:

Discuss this plan with your friend or relative. Make compromises and modifications so that you are both satisfied with it.

Many people have repressed their emotions so well that they can no longer identify how they feel. At some point in your plan, try to include this one-week exercise. For the next seven days, use the "Feelings Word List" on page 188 to help your codependent friend identify his emotions. You may want to look over the list with him at the end of the day and identify emotions he felt at various points throughout the day. Or he may want to make a copy of the list and keep it with him so he can identify his emotions more quickly.

At the end of the week, discuss these questions with him:

- Was it difficult for you to identify your feelings? Why or why not?
- What were some recurring emotions you felt during the week?
- Did you talk to anyone about your feelings? If so, how did he or she respond? If not, why not?
- How comfortable were you as you got more "in touch" with your feelings? Why?

Feelings Word List

Emotionally oriented

afraid	grateful
aggravated	grieved
agitated	happy
alarmed	horrified
amused	hurt
angry	infuriated
annoyed	irked
anxious	irritated
apprehensive	jealous
aroused	jittery
astonished	joyful
bad	joyous
bitter	jubilant
calm	lonely
comfortable	mad
concerned	melancholic
confused	merry
contented	miserable
cross	mortified
dejected	nettled
delighted	overjoyed
depressed	pleased
disappointed	rancorous
discouraged	relieved
disgruntled	resentful
disgusted	sad
dismayed	scared
displeased	shocked
distressed	sorrowful
distraught	spell-bound
disturbed	splendid
downcast	surprised
downhearted	taken aback
ecstatic	tense
elated	terrified
embarrassed	tranquil
enthralled	troubled
exhilarated	undone
frightened	uneasy
frustrated	unhappy
furious	upset
glad	vexed

Spiritually oriented

alive	indifferent
apathetic	insecure
awakened	inspired
bad	joyful
bored	joyous
bound	jubilant
committed	lonely
complacent	lost
confident	loving
courageous	moved
dead	optimistic
defeated	overwhelmed
despairing	peaceful
detached	penitent
discouraged	pessimistic
disheartened	powerful
dissatisfied	powerless
downhearted	proud
empty	redeemed
enlightened	renewed
enlivened	repentant
fearful	satisfied
free	secure
fulfilled	strong
full	sure
good guilty	thankful
helpless	touched
hopeful	trustful
hopeless	unsure
	whole

Cognitively oriented

absorbed	inquisitive
alert	interested
ambivalent	involved
appreciative	optimistic
complacent	perplexed
composed	puzzled
concerned	reluctant
confused	skeptical
curious	stimulated
engrossed	suspicious
fascinated	unconcerned
hesitant	uninterested
	unnerved

Physically oriented

alert	listless
alive	nervous
aroused	refreshed
beat	relaxed
breathless	restless
cold	run-down
comfortable	rushed
energetic	shaky
enervated	sick
enlivened	sleepy
excited	steady
exhausted	stiff
exhilarated	strong
famished	tense
fatigued	tired
full	titillated
gorged	uncomfortable
hot	unsteady
hungry	warm
hurt	weak
ill	weary
invigorated	well
jittery	wide-awake
lethargic	worn

Slang

beat	out of touch
blah	pooped
blue	psyched
broken-hearted	psyched up
burned out	run down
charged	rushed
down	shot
electrified	teed off
great	ticked off
grossed out	tight
groovy	together
hacked-off	turned off
hepped up	turned on
high	under the weather
horny	undone
hot	unglued
in touch	unhinged
keyed up	up
loose	up-tight
mellow	wasted
messed up	whipped
miffed	wiped out
mopy	wired
off	with it
on	wupped
on edge	zapped
out of it	zonked[1]

Endnotes

[1] This "Feelings Word List" is contained and more fully developed in a training module of the *Stephen Series Leader's Manual* © 1983 by Stephen Ministries. Adaptation and use is by permission of Stephen Ministries, 1325 Boland, St. Louis, Missouri 63117.

Chapter 12

The Codependent Needs . . . Separateness

During the past several years, I've been learning a lot about separateness. My own codependency once caused me to believe I had to feel what other people expected me to feel, think what they expected me to think, and act in ways they wanted me to act. Even so, not many people perceived me as being acquiescent or malleable because one of my defense mechanisms was to demand that others agree with me. I was too threatened if they didn't.

As I have learned more about my codependency, I have become more honest about my hurts, my anger, and my fears. And I have developed more of my own separate identity. Recently, a situation gave me a snapshot of my growing healthy separateness.

A friend asked my opinion about a fairly inconsequential matter. When I told him what I thought, he disagreed. Soon it became obvious that he hadn't really wanted my opinion at all. He had only asked as a bargaining chip so he could persuade me to do what he wanted me to do. Finally I said, "Ben, you asked for my opinion. I gave it to you, but you didn't value it. I feel hurt that you don't value my opinion, and I also feel that you're trying to get me to do something I've told you that I don't want to do. Excuse me, but you're on my ranch! I will make the decision I think is best."

In years past, I probably would have done whatever he had wanted because I didn't feel strong enough or secure enough to value my own opinion. But this time my refusal sparked a terrific discussion about our communication!

Another friend told me about the relationship he had with his father. "I've always done all I could do to please him. Before I made any decision, I'd wonder,

What would Dad say? If I did anything that I wasn't totally sure he'd like, I'd feel really guilty—even if he never knew about it!"

Several months of learning about codependency caused this person to see how he had lost his identity and his sense of separateness in his desire to win his father's approval. In a moment of perception and despair, he told me, "I've always felt and been what Dad wanted me to feel and to be. I don't even know how *I* really feel! I don't even know what *I* want! I don't know who *I* am!"

But he was learning.

The wife of an alcoholic lost her sense of healthy separateness. She devoted her life to fixing her husband's problems, overlooking his outbursts of abusive anger, and feeling guilty because she could never make him completely happy. He learned how to control her—to be pitiful to elicit sympathy and to use rage to intimidate her and get whatever he wanted. She spent all of her time trying to repair his ranch while he devastated hers.

The biblical principles which address separateness issues can be categorized into these groups: independence, identity, and responsibility.

Independence

Scripture states clearly that believers are to be controlled by God (Ephesians 5:18), and that we are to have self-control (Galatians 5:23), but nowhere does the Bible say that we are to be controlled by others or that we are to control others. The Bible instructs us to submit to government and authority (Romans 13:1), employers (Colossians 3:22-23), and each other (Ephesians 5:21), but submission is different from control. Submission is a *voluntary* act which has at its root the desire to please and obey God. (Note the context of submission in the passages listed.)

Control, on the other hand, is demanding, manipulative, and self-seeking. Control may come under the guise of "honoring Christ," as some people use a religious club to control and to demand acquiescence from others. But manipulative, condemning control generally produces rebellion or a crushed acquiescent spirit (or both). True submission is winsome, not manipulative or condemning. It is reasonable, not harsh. It is based on what is best for the other person, not what is best for ourselves.

For example, Paul directs: *Wives, be subject to your own husbands, as to the Lord* (Ephesians 5:22). His reasoning is not that the husband should control the wife through condemnation and manipulation. Instead, as the husband exhibits the love and self-sacrifice of Christ, the wife is won, and her submission is voluntary, not forced. Paul goes on to explain:

> *Husbands, love your wives, just as Christ also loved the church and gave Himself up for her; that He might sanctify her, having cleansed her by the washing of water with the word, that He might present to Himself the church in all her glory, having no spot or wrinkle or any such thing; but that she should be holy and blameless. So husbands ought also to love their own wives as their own bodies. He who loves his own wife loves himself; for no one ever hated his own flesh, but nourishes and cherishes it, just as Christ also does the church, because we are members of His body.*
>
> Ephesians 5:25-30

This kind of love and deference is reciprocal, not only in the marriage relationship, but in all Christian relationships: *Be subject to one another in the fear of Christ* (Ephesians 5:21). The Lord wants us to be dependent on *Him*, and to have a healthy independence rather than the bondage of pleasing people. Anything or anyone who takes the place of God in a person's life is an idol, and any compulsion to please someone at all costs is idolatry. Paul also recognized this fact when he wrote:

> *For am I now seeking the favor of men, or of God? Or am I striving to please men? If I were still trying to please men, I would not be a bond-servant of Christ.*
>
> Galatians 1:10

We can either be slaves to men and women or we can be bond-servants of Christ. We can't be both. Idolatry is severely condemned in the Scriptures, and rightly so. It is harmful to people and dishonoring to the Lord. In codependency, however, idolatry (the compulsion to please others) is rooted in hurt. Codependents need comfort, compassion, and insight, as well as repentance. Most of us already condemn ourselves for too much that we do. We don't need more condemnation from those closest to us.

Identity

The second principle related to separateness is identity. A codependent person's self-concept is based on his ability to rescue, fix, and control the emotions, attitudes, and behavior of others. He feels that he *has to* help people. When he does, he is a savior. When he can't, he's a Judas. He wants so much to be loved that he gives up his own identity in the hope of being accepted. He may, in fact, be quite successful in pleasing people so that he gets recognition and "strokes" for being "such a servant."

But his loss of identity makes him thirst for more acceptance and leads to even more erosion of identity. Of course, the lack of objectivity prevents the codependent from seeing the truth. He may have a deep reality of hurt and anger—of which he may not even be aware—coupled with loneliness, guilt, and shame. The truth will not be revealed until either someone has the love and courage to tell him (over the course of time), or he becomes so desperate that he is open to the truth.

Part of the truth he needs to recognize in regard to his identity is that God has clearly communicated that we have a new identity in Christ:

- We are deeply loved by God (1 John 4:9-10).
- We are completely forgiven by God (Romans 3:19-25).
- We are totally accepted by God (Colossians 1:19-22).
- We have been made righteous by God (2 Corinthians 5:21).
- We have been adopted by God (Ephesians 1:5).
- We have been sealed by the Holy Spirit in this new relationship (Ephesians 1:13-14).
- We are a new creation (2 Corinthians 5:17).
- We are children of God (1 John 3:1-2).

Peter further described our new identity:

But you are a chosen race, a royal priesthood, a holy nation, a
people for God's own possession, that you may proclaim the excellencies
of Him who has called you out of darkness into His marvelous light; for
you once were not a people, but now you are the people of God; you had
not received mercy, but now you have received mercy.

1 Peter 2:9-10

Scripture includes an array of metaphors which depict various aspects of our new identity in Christ and our relationship with God. Some of these are:

- Husband and wife (Ephesians 5:21-33; 2 Corinthians 11:2-3; Hosea 2:19)
- Vine and branch (John 15:1-11)
- King and ambassador (2 Corinthians 5:18-20)
- Commander and soldier (2 Timothy 2:2-4; Ephesians 6:10-20; 1 Corinthians 9:7)
- Shepherd and sheep (John 10:11; Hebrews 13:20; 1 Peter 2:25)
- Builder and building (1 Corinthians 3:9; Ephesians 2:21-22; Hebrews 11:10)
- Head and body (Colossians 1:18-24; Romans 12:5; 1 Corinthians 12:12-31)
- Master and bondservant (Romans 1:1; Philippians 1:1; Galatians 1:10)
- Father and child (Galations 4:4-7; Romans 8:15-17)
- Friends (John 15:12-17)
- Bridegroom and bride (Revelation 21:2)

These are wonderful truths, yet they can be difficult for a codependent to assimilate. To some degree he lacks the ability to perceive himself as a worthwhile, loved person. He thinks he has to earn others' acceptance by rescuing and controlling their opinions of him.

Responsibility

The third principle in regard to separateness is responsibility. Overresponsibility is a cardinal characteristic of codependency: the person looks out for the needs of other people but neglects to be responsible for his own. But this is just the opposite of the guidelines given in Scripture. Each person is supposed to be responsible to build a strong foundation in his personal life:

> *Let each one examine his own work, and then he will have reason for boasting in regard to himself alone, and not in regard to another. For each one shall bear his own load.*
>
> Galatians 6:4-5

Each of us is responsible to examine his own work and his own life, and each of us is responsible to make his own choices. Each of us will also give an account to God for the quality of our lives (1 Corinthians 3:10-15).

One time as I explained how personal responsibility is a primary factor in separateness, a lady exclaimed, "But that seems so selfish! It sounds like you're telling people to 'Look out for Number 1' instead of loving and serving others."

The very thought of taking responsibility for one's own life *can* seem selfish, especially for someone who has always defined life in terms of rescuing, fixing, and controlling. For a codependent, the worst sin in the world is selfishness! Yet the Lord wants us to develop a sense of strength in our own lives. Only then can we genuinely love others without manipulating them, give without demanding a response, and serve even when we aren't appreciated.

Codependency may seem selfless, but it isn't. The need to be loved and needed compels people to do things for others, but the motives are inherently selfish. Being responsible for ourselves, then, enables us to be less selfish, not more.

Others often try to make the codependent feel responsible for every part of the relationship, and he usually accepts the challenge. Yet this shift of responsibility can be brought to a stop with calmness and honesty. One man expected me to take all responsibility in maintaining our relationship. For weeks he intimated that I wasn't doing enough. One day I saw him at church and he blurted out, "Why haven't you called me?" I answered calmly but firmly, "George, you can pick up the phone and call *me* whenever you want to. It isn't my responsibility to call you every time you want to talk."

Dysfunctional families, to one degree or another, practice just the opposite of these separateness principles. Instead of healthy *independence*, they are at the mercy of others in an attempt to win their acceptance. Instead of a healthy *identity*, they evaluate life based on their performance and their abilities to earn respect. Instead of healthy *responsibility* for their own lives, they take care of others and expect others to take care of them. They honestly believe they are doing the right and caring thing when they live on another person's ranch.

"Who will take care of him if I don't?" one lady asked. "I'm the only one who really loves him. What would he do without me?" Codependents need to understand that loving others involves respecting their feelings and choices. And if that other person doesn't respect the codependent's separate feelings and choices, that person's control is not real love.

When a person loses his unique identity and separateness, he takes on someone else's feelings, values, opinions, desires, and behavior. This is called *enmeshment*. As I talked about this with a lady who was learning a lot about the dysfunction in her family, she suddenly realized she had hardly a single opinion or interest that was different from her mother's. She said, "We both like the same kind of houses, the same kind of furniture, and the same kind of clothes. I vote like she does. We have the same hobbies. People say we laugh alike . . . come to think of it, we even married the same kind of men!"

I asked, "How do you feel when you disagree with your mother?"

She reacted quickly, "Oh, that doesn't happen very often. But when it does, I feel very guilty and usually change my mind because she's almost always right. She respects my opinion . . . well, she respects my opinion if she agrees with it."

In his excellent book, *Inside Out* (NavPress), Dr. Larry Crabb states that all of us "thirst" for love, acceptance, and purpose. Only the Lord can satisfy that kind of thirst with His springs of "living water," but man has tried to satisfy it with substitutes such as performance, pleasing people, and denying the pain in our lives. Those who have lost their separateness (or who never developed it), however, are often not even aware of their thirst. They have subjugated their own desires, hopes, feelings, and opinions, and they have taken on these values from other people, hoping to win love and acceptance. But then they don't even know what they want. They aren't in touch with their thirst.

You can help your codependent relative or friend take the next step in experiencing separateness. Help him *identify* the times when he is "ranch hopping," *detach* so he can understand why he is doing that, and *decide* to take the next step toward healthy separateness. If you play a primary role in his life, you can provide the warmth and encouragement, as well as the insight, that he needs before he can value himself and develop separateness. If you are in a support role, you can have a powerful impact as you value his choices without manipulating him. Also, it will be very helpful if you are honest about your own desires and if you make your own choices as an example for him.

Help The Other Person Identify
How His Separateness Has Been Hindered

If you have worked through the sections on perception and love (Chapters 10 and 11) with your relative or friend, then he has probably already learned a lot about his lack of separateness. Help him see how others have manipulated him and not valued his own emotions and choices. Ask questions like:

- How do you feel when someone you care for disagrees with you? How do you respond? Do you change your feelings or behavior to suit him? Why?
- What cues tell you if someone likes what you've said or done? How do you respond when you see those cues?
- What are similarities and differences between your tastes and the person who influences you the most?
- How do you respond to criticism?

Sarcasm?	Silence?
Abuse?	Appreciation?
Being needed?	Praise?

- How do you react when someone tries to manipulate you? (Some people who are manipulated give in right away. Others react in the opposite manner, demanding that their opinions be heard, their feelings be valued, and their behavior be accepted. Help your codependent friend or relative identify his response.)
- To summarize: In what ways do you let people on your ranch? What is the effect of their being there?

You can also help the other person identify *his* control and manipulation of others. Ask him:

- How do you treat people who agree with you? How about people who disagree with you? Do you try to change how others feel or act? If so, how?
- Do you use any of these to control others? If so, how?

Criticism?	Sarcasm?
Silence?	Abuse?
Appreciation?	Being needed?
Praise?	

- Is there anyone whom you regard very highly at one point but get very hurt or angry with at another? Who is it? Describe a recent situation. (When a person lacks a sense of separateness, he tends to see people's character as black or white.)

The questions in the previous two chapters may also be helpful as you encourage your friend or relative to come to grips with his overresponsibility toward others and his irresponsibility about his own life.

Help Him Detach

As a codependent grows healthier and stronger, he will become more aware of his own identity and of his "thirst." He will realize that it is OK to want. It's OK to be disappointed. He will be more secure in his separateness. He can be right without being cocky, and wrong without being defensive. He won't feel so threatened by others' disapproval, and he won't feel as inflated by others' respect or appreciation. The process of getting to this point, however, requires a good honest look at the realities of enmeshment and an analysis of the next step to take. Help your friend or relative detach and understand the separateness issues by discussing:

- Why do you let people on your ranch?
- Who do you keep off your ranch at all costs?
- What is the condition of your ranch right now?
- What do you need to do to get people off your ranch?
- What can you do to reclaim the land, rebuild the fences, and rehang the gates?
- Under what conditions will you invite someone onto your ranch in the future?
- When and why would you ask someone to leave?
- Why do you go onto others' ranches? What do you usually do there?
- What is the condition of those ranches right now?
- How can you help other people be more responsible for their own ranches? Be specific.
- Under what condition will you go on their ranches again?
- When will you leave?
- Does taking care of your own ranch seem selfish to you? Why or why not?

This ranch metaphor has been very helpful to me. I can visualize myself in years past hiding down among the cottonwoods in the creek bed because I had let some people burn my barn, steal my cattle, and ruin my crops. Others had come on my ranch to fix it up, paint the house, and hoe the garden. And I would often leave the cottonwoods to go to someone else's ranch to take care of their needs for them. Detaching helped me break my habit of ranch-hopping.

Detachment involves stepping away in order to be more objective and to make good decisions. We can learn to detach emotionally even when we are in a difficult situation or with someone who has controlled or condemned us. But sometimes we need to detach physically, to separate ourselves from someone who has dominated us. This separation gives us some "breathing room" and an opportunity to develop strength, stability, and a sense of confidence. We can relate to the person with more maturity the next time we are with him.

We can take a drive, go to the library, or take a walk for a while. We can take a couple of days from time to time to replenish emotional reserves and regain a sense of separateness and identity. We can take a sabbatical from a relationship (such as not calling a parent for a month or more). The type of physical detachment depends on such factors as: the type of relationship (spouse, child, parent, friend, employee, etc.), the level of need in your life, and the level of control exercised by the other person. I am not advocating a permanent physical separation (like divorce). Talk to a wise friend or counselor who can help you determine the best plan.

Physical detachment is, then, an aid to help develop strength and perception so we can more easily detach emotionally whenever we need to do so. All of us need to learn to detach emotionally and remain objective in the middle of conversations and situations. Many of us also need to detach physically. What kind of detachment is appropriate for you?

Help The Other Person Decide

The codependent is fighting two battles in regard to this separateness issue. One is inside himself—a struggle to be separate and independent. The other battle is dealing with the expectations of other people. For example, a codependent in the savior mode has caused others to expect him to solve their problems. They are conditioned to his patterns of rescuing and overresponsibility. When the savior suddenly decides not to rescue, the others usually don't appreciate his separateness!

As in the previous two chapters, decisions to pursue separateness center on reading, relationships, and risks.

Reading—Articles, tapes, and books on separateness can be a great encouragement to someone who is learning the limits of his responsibilities. So can Bible studies on identity. As we have already seen, *The Search for Significance* and *Your Parents and You* (both co-published by Rapha Publishing/Word, Inc.) are good resources for a codependent friend or relative.

Relationships—Your affirmation of the other person's values, his feelings, and opinions will provide the environment he needs to take steps toward healthy independence. It is ironic that a person's degree of separateness usually parallels his being supported by someone who genuinely cares about him. The deeper the bond of love, the more secure and separate he can be.

You can help your friend or relative set limits and take specific steps in the process of experiencing independence. Some of these statements (from my *Codependency* book) might help him set limits in his relationships. Discuss with the person some specific conditions where he might use each of the statements:

- This is what I will do. This is what I won't do.
- I will not take this kind of behavior anymore.
- I'm not responsible for his happiness.
- I refuse to be manipulated.
- I'm sorry, I wish I could help you, but I can't.
- Why did you say that to me? Do you know how I feel when you say things like that?
- I don't want to talk about this.
- I want to talk about this.

Some of these statements may seem harsh to the person, but it will take a clear, definitive thought process to overcome the sticky goo left behind from patterns of manipulation.

Be patient with him. Remember that he has seen life from a different perspective for a long time. Perception rarely changes suddenly. And with more accurate perception comes the reality of hurt and anger, a revelation that can be very threatening to him. Real progress is possible, however, as you provide honesty, love, and a good model of positive separateness.

Risks—The other person's palms may sweat and his voice may quiver the first several (hundred) times he says no, is honest about his feelings, or states his opinion to someone. The transition from being controlled to becoming separate is something like letting go of a grizzly bear so you can step out on a frozen lake where you suspect the ice is very thin. You finally realize that you need to let go, but you aren't sure about risking the next step on the ice. Yet as you get more assured that the ice will hold you, you are overjoyed to be stepping away from the bear.

These realizations don't happen all at once. Deceptions and repressed emotions require a lot of time to work out. Every new insight seems like the "most significant one in the world," and it is—up to that point! Most people, however, will continue to make new discoveries about themselves even after months or years of the healing process. The first steps are crucial and they give new freedom and independence...but there's much more to come.

Summary

Look over this chapter again and write out a plan to help your codependent friend or relative identify, detach, and decide as he learns to experience separateness.

How to Help Him Identify:

How to Help Him Detach:

How to Help Him Decide:

Discuss this plan with your friend or relative. Make compromises and modifications until you are both satisfied with it.

Chapter 13

Beginning the Process

By now you have discovered that a codependent person needs perception, love, and separateness. But how can you help your relative or friend begin the healing process and discover these things? How can you help him overcome his two most significant barriers: denial and bargaining? Perhaps the first question to consider at this point is: Why does a person unconsciously develop denial as a means of blocking out pain?

As we have described in the earlier chapters of this book, a child has a God-given need for a stable and loving home environment. When warmth and love aren't provided to a significant degree, it shakes the foundation of the child's life. It is simply too threatening for a child to be objective about his parents' failures and his own pain. He doesn't have the perception, the emotional strength, or other strong relationships to enable him to cope with the reality in his family.

So, a child learns to believe that his family is "normal," that his parents and siblings are "the way they should be," and that any problems which occur are because something is wrong with *him*, not them. Day after day and year after year, this misperception is reinforced. Seeing reality, feeling the pain and anger, and talking about the problem are condemned, not encouraged. It is a tight web. A strong grip. A deceptive blindness.

So of the many and varied reasons that people in these families remain in a state of denial, two reasons seem to stand out: (1) a lack of knowledge, and (2) fear. Usually both of these are in evidence.

Before we look more specifically at how you can help your friend or relative overcome denial and bargaining, let's look at two factors which need to pervade your relationship with him.

Scalpels and Hugs

Two factors which are instrumental in the early stages of a person's growth (and indeed, throughout the entire process) are truth and love. Truth about ourselves, others, and God can cut like a scalpel through the tough layers of defense mechanisms so that we begin to perceive and experience reality in our lives. The warmth of loving relationships provides the acceptance and encouragement needed to be honest and to take the next steps.

There are many good books, Bible studies, counselors, and other resources which can help us see the painful truth about our lives and the wonderful reality of God's love and strength. Again, one excellent resource is *The Search for Significance* (Rapha Publishing/Word, Inc.), which exposes many of the lies which we tend to believe and presents corollary truths from God's Word to help people begin to see reality.

Referring to this book, one man told me, "Until I saw it in black and white, I never realized how much I live for other people's approval!"

A college student remarked, "I've tried to get all the honors I could so that my family and friends would accept me. Now I understand why I've done that, and I understand more how God loves and accepts me unconditionally. I have a long way to go, but I'm getting there."

A woman who had been depressed for years said, "I have had so much anger inside, but I thought I was normal. God has used *The Search for Significance* to help me see how much of my life has been lived in bitterness and blaming myself and others."

Exposure of previous lies seems to trigger insight for many people. Examining these deceptions seems to "turn on the lights," though even then, a person may not see clearly at first. When I first began to study them, I could easily see that I had problems with rejection and failure, but I couldn't recognize other problems. Over a year later, I saw for the first time that blame and shame had been just as much a part of my life as the fears of rejection and failure. I simply didn't see them at first. As the years have passed, I've continued to see more situations where I am influenced by these deceptions. The scalpel keeps cutting deeper as I grow.

But a person probably won't allow the scalpel to cut very deeply at all if he is not involved in some affirming relationships. Reality is just too painful to handle on one's own. A person who is hurt by others, depressed, or driven needs someone to "be there" as he takes the first steps to be honest about his life. Each of the people quoted in the previous paragraphs were able to discover the truth because they were in the context of meaningful relationships. One was in a small group Bible study, one met with a friend every week, and one saw a Christian counselor.

God made us to be relational people. Our deepest pain was probably caused by people, and fear of additional pain often keeps us from pursuing relationships. But affirmation, love, honesty, and encouragement are vital ingredients to our progress and health.

A person needs to experience warmth and affirmation before he is open to the scalpel of truth. Without genuine love, that scalpel should never be used. Yet healing takes place when love is consistent and the truth is used in an artful and timely manner. With these things in mind, let's now examine the hurdle of denial.

Overcoming Denial

Perhaps your friend or relative wants help and is far beyond the initial stages of the healing process, yet is stuck firmly in the mud of denial. Some people start the process by reading a book, getting some insight, and then finding a relationship that helps them continue. Others begin a relationship first, unwilling to look at an article or have a conversation about their needs until they are sure of being loved and accepted.

As you contemplate talking to the other person about his codependency, be sure to find a neutral place in a calm, unhurried environment. Communicate that you care, then tell him, "Here are some things I've observed...."

Describe the characteristics of codependency, referring to the inner hurt that precipitates these feelings and behaviors. Don't demand an instant response. He may be defensive, or he may get depressed. Affirm him. Tell him of his strengths. Focus on hurts, not wrongs; causes, not effects. Ask him to read *Codependency* or some similar resource. No matter how calm and loving you are, he may feel attacked by you. He may suppose that he can't afford to be wrong, so your confrontation is a tremendous threat to him. Don't overreact to his defensiveness. Be calm, gentle, clear, and firm.

In the black-or-white outlook of codependency, someone in the savior mode may not see any need to change. One lady was so affirmed by her overly responsible rescuing that she couldn't understand how it could possibly be wrong! Or someone in the Judas mode may see the need to change, but he may not believe he can ever feel good about himself or develop healthy relationships with others. Most codependents will alternate between the two, feeling indispensable at one point and worthless at another. Their vacillation can be very confusing—for them and for the people who care about them.

The codependent needs to realize that sooner or later he *will* face risks— whether or not he starts the healing process. The risks of overcoming codependency are the probability of experiencing latent hurt, anger, and fear throughout a prolonged period of healing. But the risks of not going through this process are a clouded and distorted perception of his self-concept, his relationship with God, his relationships with parents, spouse, children, siblings, friends, and employer, and every other aspect of his life. He will never have his own identity and he will be unable to experience or express love.

Your codependent friend or relative probably has a great fear of being alone in this process. He may fear that your very mention of his behavior means that you are rejecting him. He needs your affirmation and constant love as you continue to be honest.

If you are in a supportive role in your relative's or friend's life, your relationship with him probably has a pattern of rescuing. He may be used to rescuing you. You may be accustomed to rescuing him. So now you need to set limits. Here are a few which may be appropriate:

- Don't rescue him anymore.
- Let him make his own decisions. Don't tell him how to feel, think, or act.
- Don't let him rescue you anymore. Don't let him tell you how to think, feel, or act.
- Be honest. Be patient.

- Communicate using "I" words. It is better to say, "I feel hurt when you..." instead of, "You are so mean!"

The person may need time, space, and distance from you. It hurts, but it may be necessary. He may also test your commitment to see if you choose to listen or condemn, love or reject, be honest or lie, be patient or angry, be open or defensive. As James encouraged us: *Let everyone be quick to hear, slow to speak, and slow to anger* (James 1:19).

The first steps for your friend or relative are crucial, but you can't make him take them. All you can do is provide a loving, safe environment where you are honest with him. You can encourage him to take these steps, but it's his responsibility to act. People usually don't understand and respond the first time—or the first several times—they hear about emotional needs. Their defense mechanisms are often very strong. But sooner or later, the time will come to listen, to understand, and to begin the process of healing.

Many years ago, a friend talked to me about some hurts in my life. I listened carefully, thanked him for his honesty and concern, and promptly wrote him off! Maybe he should have talked to me again. He didn't. Maybe I should have understood the reality of what he was saying about me. I didn't. Several years later, I learned more about the hurt and defense mechanisms in my life, and then I remembered that previous conversation with my friend. I guess the timing just wasn't right.

When I talk to some people about the hurts in their lives, the Lord seems to have prepared them for that precise moment. Things "click," and they seem to enter the healing process running on all cylinders. But usually the Lord uses a combination of events and people over a long period of time so that the "lights come on" fairly slowly. Some codependents go through years of solid input and gracious communication—lots of scalpels and hugs—but they still don't see reality in their lives...at least not yet!

Mary's experience is typical. She had grown up in a home where her father worked 60-70 hours a week and her mother was hooked on prescription drugs. Mary became a Christian in her 20s. She learned a lot and seemed to grow quickly, but some things seemed to plague her in her relationship with the Lord. A friend in a

Bible study had lunch with her one day and remarked that Mary seemed to be a driven, overly intense person. Mary was defensive and said, "The Lord wants us to do things with excellence, you know. He doesn't appreciate us being sloppy or lazy!" The friend was intimidated and never brought up the subject again.

Later, another of Mary's friends read an article about codependency. She sent Mary a copy and a book on the subject. Mary wondered why her friend would send her such materials. The friend asked about it several times and Mary made some lame excuses. When she finally read the book, Mary told her friend, "Well, maybe there were a couple of things that related to me."

Her friend replied enthusiastically, "I've learned so much from this book, Mary. And when I read it, I just knew you could identify with almost every point!"

Mary was not encouraged. Her friend's high enthusiasm and exhortation made her wonder if there was more to the problem of codependency than she realized.

Two years later, Mary found herself in a Bible study at her church. One of the women in the study was very open about her family and the hurts and fears she had struggled to overcome. As the weeks passed, Mary began to realize that she had experienced the same struggles, but she had thought they were a normal part of life. "Doesn't everybody feel that way?" she asked.

Slowly, Mary began to see her life more objectively. Today she is in the middle of the healing process. Sometimes she wishes she had never seen that open, vulnerable woman in her Bible study because then she wouldn't have started the painful process. But she sees progress. It's slow, but it's there.

We can't push people to respond. We *can* invite them, create a climate that encourages the person, be honest about our hurts and fears, and describe our own struggles. We can address the many issues that cloud a codependent's life and hinder perception—financial needs, intense relational problems, overwhelming problems at work, depression, or any other of a myriad of problems. And as we do, we need to recognize that a lack of perception has a spiritual dimension, as well. Pray that the Lord will cause *light [to] shine out of darkness* (2 Corinthians 4:6) so the rescuer can see his need as well as the provision of the real Savior. Be patient. Provide a good environment. And wait for the Lord's timing in the codependent's life.

Overcoming Bargaining

When a codependent first comes to grips with the dysfunction in his family and the damage in his own life, he may respond by bargaining. One man remarked, "Then what can I do to get my father to love me?" A lady said, "I'll do anything for my parents. I just want them to accept me." Bargaining is a common phenomenon, but it severely hinders progress. It is the outgrowth of the person's limited, incomplete perception.

Typically, a person who bargains is still desperately hoping that the people who have hurt him the most will give him the love he wants so much. It is extremely difficult to give up that hope. One man told me that for three and a half years he clung to the hope that his alcoholic parents would meet his deepest needs. Then he realized that they would probably never love him the way he wanted to be loved. He finally gave up on his unrealistic hope.

Even though a person in the bargaining stage clings to the hope of being loved by the ones who have deeply hurt him, he is usually very angry at them as well (for not loving him). In this stage, he can be terribly confused. Sometimes he is bitterly angry. Other times he is ashamed and guilty for being angry at those who have hurt him.

You can help him deal with his anger—and possibly advance past the bargaining stage—by helping him assign appropriate responsibility for offenses. Being codependent, his assignment of blame will tend to be either black or white. He will either blame others with a vengeance or not blame them at all (even if they have committed great offenses). Sometimes a person in this stage will be overwhelmed at the hurt inflicted by someone else and perhaps irrational in his fury at the offenses. Or he may feel sorry for the offender and excuse the other person's offense: "Poor Dad, he couldn't help the way he treated me. He was doing the best he could."

Parents, spouses, and siblings should be responsible to love, accept, and forgive. A child in a dysfunctional family isn't responsible to figure out why the parent doesn't love him. It is not the child's responsibility to protect and provide for the dependent parent, yet that is precisely what codependency is: a reversal of roles and responsibilities. Assigning appropriate responsibility will help your friend or relative affix the right responsibilities to the right persons for the right reasons.

As you talk about these things with your friend or relative, help him see what each person was (and is) responsible to be and do toward him. Also help him define his responsibilities toward others. As he assigns appropriate responsibility to them, he can assign appropriate blame as well (not too much or too little). Instead of taking it all on himself, he can begin to feel *appropriate* hurt and anger which leads to appropriate forgiveness and healing. And he will move several steps farther in his progress.

A person in these early stages of overcoming codependency often experiences wide swings in feelings and behavior. As the cap is taken off his emotions, he may feel more hurt, anger, and fear than he ever thought possible. He may become afraid of the intensity of his emotions and put the cap back on until he has more courage to experiment again with the feelings. He may also feel more joy, freedom, and love than ever before. He may cry for the first time in years. He may feel loved and comforted for the first time ever. He may ask hundreds of questions. He will be vulnerable to bad advice because he doesn't have the wisdom that will come as the process continues.

These wide swings are understandable. Don't try to clamp them. Instead, help the friend or relative see that the sudden surges of emotions are perfectly understandable for someone who has repressed them for years. No, he won't be that way the rest of his life. After a while, the emotions won't be as volatile as they are now.

The beginning of this process is a vital, if awkward, step toward spiritual, emotional, and relational healing. Be patient, and be sure to apply plenty of scalpels and hugs.

Summary

1. What are some aspects of truth ("the scalpel") that can help your codependent friend or relative?

2. What are some aspects of warmth ("hugs") that can help your codependent friend or relative?

3. How can these be blended?

4. What is your perception of the timing factor for your friend or relative beginning the process or taking the next step in his life?

5. What are some ways you (and he) can tell if he is bargaining?

Chapter 14

Continuing the Process

As the codependent progresses through the healing process, his heightened emotions will become less extreme. The ups and downs while becoming less pronounced, will still exist. In fact, he may even begin to recognize patterns or cycles in his responses to people and situations.

In this chapter we will examine some of the cycles a person may experience as he gets farther into the healing process. We will also look at some other very important factors in your friend or relative's progress, including forgiveness, fresh insight about codependency, and the reality of spiritual conflict. First, let's examine some of the cycles a person can experience.

Cycles

Recently I have been learning about how I communicate with people—not just with words, but with expressions and pictures as well. A couple of weeks ago I tried to get Taylor, my son, to pick up the 8,742,323,974 baseball cards which are all over (and I mean *all over*) his room. (I didn't know they made baseball card carpets!) Our family was going somewhere soon, so I tried to "encourage" him to pick them up a little more quickly. Then I left him to his task.

A funny thing happened, though. When I walked back into his room a bit later, he was reading the cards one by one! I told him that we didn't have time to look at the batting averages and ERA's of each player. My tone became more stern, so this time I was sure he would make Mr. Clean look like a slob!

I was wrong. I walked back into his room just before it was time to leave. He was carefully analyzing the skills of each player in each position for each year of his career! I glared at Taylor and told him how disappointed I was.

Then I suddenly realized that my expression was harsh and foreboding. I could imagine how my face showed anger, and I thought of how my expression and tone of voice communicated condemnation, not loving discipline. I realized that I was hurting my son deeply.

After apologies to Taylor, I spent some time reflecting on my harsh communication. It hurt me to realize how quickly my emotions could get out of control. It hurt a lot. But this incident became an important step in my communication with my son and in my understanding of the anger buried inside of me. The reflection made me determine to break the habit of responding to others' errors with condemnation.

Insight (about ourselves, God, other people, the past, or whatever) sometimes reveals repressed hurt or anger. Yet through the sudden pain can emerge a determination to make good choices and take the next step toward health. And that step of valuing ourselves, saying no to manipulation, setting limits, being honest with someone, or serving for the right reason often provides even more insight. This positive cycle of growth may be diagrammed like this:

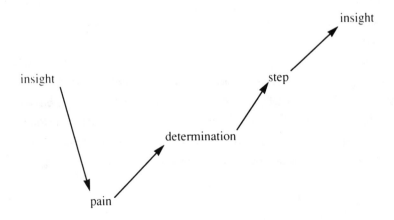

A flash of insight may also provide immediate strength and encouragement even in the midst of pain. A person may suddenly realize that he is valued by someone else. He may discover that he is growing in his capacity to feel his emotions, think independently, and make his own decisions. That strength enables him to take yet another step, which may reveal even more hurt he had not been aware of before. But he gains more insight from the experience of the new pain.

Many times the affirmation of my wife, my children, or my friends has helped me believe that I have value and that somebody cares more about who I am than what I can do for them. Those times have given me strength and courage to keep going, and often the Lord uses those opportunities to reveal another area of my hidden hurt or fear. Without the insight provided by these people and the Lord, however, I wonder if I could ever take those steps. Without help from others, the cycle might look like this:

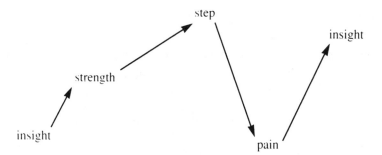

People sometimes wonder why some insights make them feel so good and others make them feel so bad. As we see truth about ourselves and we feel someone's genuine care for us, it may feel like a cool drink of water on a hot day! But other times we can be overwhelmed with anger, fear, or hurt as we see clearly the stark realities of our lives. Such widely varied responses to the insights we gain can seem very disturbing at first, but we must understand that they are a normal part of the process.

When your friend or relative first learns about codependency, he usually wants to leave behind his dysfunctional behavior and go straight to health, peace, love, and happiness. He doesn't realize that to climb the mountain, he has to go into the valley first.

Long's Peak is a picturesque mountain in Rocky Mountain National Park. A long and difficult trail leads up to the top, and hundreds of hikers make the trek every year. If you stand at one of the lookout points on Trail Ridge Highway, you can see the mountain in the distance, but the trail to get there leads into the valley right in front of you. After hiking for many miles, through many valleys and over several ridges, you finally ascend the mountain. At an elevation of about 13,500 feet, you cross The Keyhole, a narrow ridge that leads to the next section of the trail. At that point, with the peak only about 500 feet away (in elevation), many tired hikers' hearts sink because they have to climb down into The Trough, which drops about 150 feet in elevation. The last part of the trail, The Homestretch, must be traversed on hands and knees over slabs of granite. The climb had been difficult before The Keyhole, but The Trough and The Homestretch are both emotionally and physically taxing.

The path from codependency to health is much like the trail to the top of Long's Peak. Many of us would prefer a helicopter ride to the top of life's mountain. We don't ever want to go down. We want to continually go up! But life is full of cycles. The way of healing is to come to grips with the repressed hurt, anger, and fear that has blocked our growth. We have to enter the Valley of Identified Repression before the climb begins. And even when we are making real progress on the mountain, we will come to frequent troughs on the trail. Though we seem to be going down, the trail will eventually lead upward again.

It is natural to want that helicopter ride to the health, hope, and intimacy at the summit. No one enjoys the tedious foot trail down into the valleys.

It takes courage to go into the valley. It requires the affirmation and help of someone who has been there before us. Going down isn't easy. It takes strength. We must get stronger to go deeper. But then we can begin our ascent to a point higher than ever before. Our trek includes the many ups and downs of the cycles of insights, pain, hope, and renewal. When the cycles are combined with the mountain illustration, the diagram of our progress looks like this:

As I have experienced this process myself, I have often come to points where I thought, *It's over now. I'm on top. I'm finally free from the pain!* I expected to be happy for the rest of my life! But after a while, the Lord would show me a deeper sense of pain or anger. The first few times (Make that the first *many* times!), I got discouraged at these new revelations. Yet eventually I began to be more realistic about the process. It is long and slow, just like a mountain trail. Today I still don't enjoy discovering new levels of repressed anger or fear in my life, but I'm not as surprised or discouraged when they emerge. I know God will get me through it and make me stronger because of the process. The Lord is kind not to show me all of my hidden problems at once! He is patient. I can be, too. Experiencing the pain of the past will allow me to experience freedom and love during the present and future. It's not an easy path, but it's worth the trip.

Forgiveness

Typically, a person will experience the truth of God's love, forgiveness, and acceptance only as deeply as he has experienced the reality of pain in his life. If he is only superficially objective, then he will experience only superficial love, comfort, and forgiveness (though he may think this is all there is). As he gains a deeper sense of reality, he will also be able to feel a deeper sense of comfort, love, and forgiveness.

The ability to forgive others is often an indicator of the depth of the person's experience of reality. Cindy asked if she could talk to me about her father. "When you talked about forgiveness tonight," she said, "I was confused. I've forgiven my father for all he did to me. I know I have. And I've worked through all of my feelings, but I still hate him. What's wrong with me?"

I asked a few questions about her father. He had neglected her, and his only contact seemed to be through his verbal abuse. Cindy had been deeply hurt by him.

"Cindy," I told her, "you *have* forgiven your father. I appreciate your desire to do that. But you haven't yet felt all the pain you repressed, so your forgiveness is only as deep as the pain you have allowed yourself to feel. That's why you're confused about forgiveness."

I explained that two things are necessary before a person can genuinely forgive other people. The first is that we need to experience the pain of the offense. Others' wrongs toward us hurt! If we repress those feelings to lessen the hurt, it confuses our forgiveness. We believe we have forgiven the offender, but we still harbor resentment.

If we are open and honest about the pain, however, we will know exactly why we are forgiving the other person. David modeled this honesty about his hurt and anger in his psalms. Christ didn't deny His feelings, either. Jesus felt anger at those who rejected Him, fear at the imminent crucifixion, and hurt that His followers abandoned Him. We need to be honest as well. It may take a lot of time to uncover previously repressed emotions, but we should do so for our forgiveness of others to follow the progress of our objectivity about their offenses.

The second necessity for genuine forgiveness is a deep appreciation for Christ's forgiveness of us. Our forgiveness of others reflects the depth of our grasp of our own forgiveness. The more we realize that we have been completely forgiven of our bitterness, pride, malice, and neglect of others, then we will be increasingly able—and motivated—to forgive those who hurt us. Paul encourages us: *Be kind to one another, tender-hearted, forgiving each other, just as God in Christ also has forgiven you* (Ephesians 4:32).

Those who have been hurt deeply need to forgive the people who hurt them. Such forgiveness is often the foundation for further growth. But that forgiveness must be based on both an honest appraisal of the depth of the hurt caused by the offense and a deep experience of the forgiveness of Christ.

Insights about Codependency

As your friend or relative grows in the areas of perception, love, and separateness, he will begin to notice a number of paradoxes and insights about his codependency. Some will come through painful and slow realization. Others may be "Aha!" experiences. His "new" insights may be things you have known for a long time. Many have already been discussed in this book. They may include the perceptions that:

- Codependents help others not because they want to serve, but to try to fulfill deep needs in their own lives.
- They live for compliments, but when they are praised they won't accept compliments (because they don't believe them).
- They may be very perceptive about other people, but not about themselves or their families.
- They say that they hate to be controlled, yet they are easily manipulated.
- They are overly responsible about others, but irresponsible about themselves. (They live on each other's ranches.)
- They can appear very self-assured and confident, but it is a facade which hides their fear of being weak.
- They may have wonderful social skills but feel very lonely.
- They may be outwardly tough and demanding but inwardly feel deeply hurt.
- They defend and excuse the ones who have hurt them the most, but blame and condemn themselves instead.
- They may feel like an indispensable savior one minute and a shameful Judas the next.
- They think they love, give, and serve, but they don't know what it's like to experience those things deeply.
- They may indulge in endless self-pity rather than make decisions that will make their lives better.

These are just a few of the many ironies that a codependent begins to recognize as he emerges from his compulsive, overly responsible rescuing. Your friend or relative may come up with a number of additional observations.

The Necessity of Relationships

A person needs two kinds of relationships in order to develop emotional, relational, and spiritual health: (1) a strong relationship with God, and (2) strong relationships with people. Volumes have been—and can still be—written about man's need for God. We are people who are desperately deceived, desperately sinful, and desperately needy. We need a Savior. We need Jesus Christ. He alone is the source of forgiveness, life, hope, love, and peace.

To communicate this truth to us, God has provided two primary sources: the Bible and the Holy Spirit (though government, law, and nature could also be included on our list). And to help us experience this truth, He has structured two primary environments: the biological family and the family of God. God intends for the family to model and impart His nature during a child's critical formative years. But when the family fails in its responsibility, we still have other believers to help us overcome the deficiencies and deceptions of the past. It is God's desire that we experience the reality of His presence and purposes.

People need each other. We need others to encourage, reprove, exhort, comfort, teach, love, and pray for us. Paul describes both the intricate workings and the purposes of our relationships with one another:

> *Until we all attain to the unity of the faith, and of the knowledge of the Son of God, to a mature man, to the measure of the stature which belongs to the fullness of Christ.*
>
> *As a result, we are no longer to be children, tossed here and there by waves, and carried about by every wind of doctrine, by the trickery of men, by craftiness in deceitful scheming;*
>
> *But speaking the truth in love, we are to grow up in all aspects into Him, who is the head, even Christ.*
>
> *From whom the whole body, being fitted and held together by that which every joint supplies, according to the proper working of each individual part, causes the growth of the body for the building up of itself in love.*
>
> Ephesians 4:13-16

The goal—for ourselves and each other—is maturity in knowing Christ. One hindrance is the deception that comes from immaturity. But "speaking the truth in love" stimulates growth and development so we can relate to each other in healthy, productive, stimulating, Christ-honoring ways. The issue of relationships within the body of Christ is so important that Paul devotes large sections of each of his letters to enhance these relationships.

People from dysfunctional families know less about healthy relationships than other people (and are more in need of them). Deception, abuse, neglect, and manipulation have scarred their lives. In an article about the need for authentic relationships James M. Houston wrote:

> *When authentic spiritual guidance reveals the reality of human sin, and the relevance of Christ's lordship and redemption to our emotions and our minds, then it will help expose the intrinsically self-deceiving character of sin in our lives....*
>
> *If sin is self-deceiving, then I need a soul friend to give me insights into the ways I am deceived, or insensitive, or hardened by sin within me. I cannot do it alone. Self-examination can only take me so far. I need others to help expose and help me understand where sin would deceive and confuse me.*[1]

Houston describes people in authentic Christian relationships as "soul friends." He continued to describe the power and the insight these relationships have to change lives:

> *Often our soul friends can show us the ecology of evil within us, how a particular childhood wound, or fixation of emotion, or emotional frame of mind, have brought the addictions that now enthrall us, coloring and distorting all we do and are. It may be that only the courage and wisdom of true soul friends can expose the ambitions and compulsions that lie behind our addictions to ministry, to pleasing everybody, or to "being in the limelight."*[2]

Spiritual Conflict

One thing common to all people in Christian relationships is the experience of spiritual conflict. All of us are under attack from the enemy's lies and schemes.

Hurting people from dysfunctional families are particularly susceptible to deception. We need to be alert and aware of this conflict: *Be of sober spirit, be on the alert. Your adversary, the devil, prowls about like a roaring lion, seeking someone to devour* (1 Peter 5:8).

Many believers go to extremes in regard to spiritual conflict. Some don't acknowledge the reality of demonic forces at all and try to explain everything in rational and material terms. Others believe that *everything* is explainable in terms of demonic and angelic forces.

In recent years, Bible scholars like Dr. Neil Anderson (chairman of the Department of Practical Theology of Talbot Theological Seminary) and Dr. C. Fred Dickason (chairman of the Department of Systematic Theology at Moody Bible Institute) have brought clarity and balance to this often misunderstood issue.

It is important that we—and our growing friends or relatives—have a balanced understanding of these issues. Though we won't be able to go into the detail and depth that Dr. Anderson and Dr. Dickason have gone, let's briefly examine five principles they have put together regarding spiritual conflict.

Principle #1—Acknowledge Spiritual Conflict as a Reality

Jesus didn't mince words when He rebuked the religious leaders who opposed him. He recognized the source of their opposition:

> *"You are of your father the devil, and you want to do the desires of your father. He was a murderer from the beginning, and does not stand in the truth, because there is no truth in him. Whenever he speaks a lie, he speaks from his own nature; for he is a liar, and the father of lies"*
> John 8:44

Throughout Scripture, the writers document the reality of spiritual conflict. It was never in question to them. (See also Daniel 10:10-14 and Ephesians 6:10-13.)

Jesus Himself made many references to Satan's purposes, including the one in John 10:10: *The thief comes only to steal, and kill, and destroy.* In many families Satan accomplishes that purpose through neglect, abuse, and manipulation. The environment of such hurtful relationships effectively steals any sense of self-worth, kills the ability to experience healthy separateness and intimacy, and destroys the joy of life Christ desires for us. The evil present in these families is not contained within the destructive acts and absence of nurturing. The evil becomes a dynamic in the person's thoughts and beliefs which distorts his perception, blinds him to the truth, and perpetuates itself.

In some families this evil is manifested by neglect—through absence of time, attention, and nurturing. People who have experienced physical and emotional neglect often describe the "terrible emptiness" which is "like a vast desert" that leaves them "lonely, hopeless, desperate, and confused."

In other families, a combination of self-pity and control sends double messages. Someone may say, "Oh, I don't know what I'd do without you!" to elicit the pity and rescuing of others. But when the rescuer has been drawn close, he is often condemned if he doesn't do *exactly* what the other person expects. He is often condemned even when he does *far more* than was requested. This combination of pity and control makes a person vulnerable and open to the dependent person's attacks. Like Satan in the Garden, the promise of bliss (in this case, acceptance) is followed by harsh condemnation and tragic consequences. Sadly, many people in these families never gain objective perception so they can make good choices to step away and develop emotional, spiritual, and relational health.

The evil in these dysfunctional family systems produces to one degree or another, a blend of hopelessness, desperation to achieve success and please others, and continued denial of the reality of the problem.

Principle #2—Acknowledge Christ's Ultimate Power and Authority

Though the demonic forces of darkness are strong, Christ is much more powerful. Paul wrote that Jesus is

> *...far above all rule and authority and power and dominion, and every name that is named, not only in this age, but also in the one to come.*

And [God] put all things in subjection under His feet, and gave Him
as head over all things to the church,
  Which is His body, the fulness of Him who fills all in all.
                                                    Ephesians 1:21-23

Paul also assured the believers in Philippi of Christ's supreme authority:

Therefore also God highly exalted Him, and bestowed on Him the
name which is above every name,
  That at the name of Jesus every knee should bow, of those who are
in heaven, and on earth, and under the earth,
  And that every tongue should confess that Jesus Christ is Lord, to
the glory of God the Father.
                                                    Philippians 2:9-11

Christ's death conquered both sin and the power of the enemy:

When He had disarmed the rulers and authorities, He made a
public display of them, having triumphed over them through Him.
                                                    Colossians 2:15

Principle #3—Learn The Schemes of the Enemy

Paul knew that victory in Christ came only as a result of spiritual conflict. And any good soldier discovers as much as he can about the strategies of his enemy. Paul offers sound advice in preparing for battle:

Finally, be strong in the Lord, and in the strength of His might.
  Put on the full armor of God, that you may be able to stand firm
against the schemes of the devil.

For our struggle is not against flesh and blood, but against the
rulers, against the powers, against the world forces of this darkness,
against the spiritual forces of wickedness in the heavenly places.

Ephesians 6:10-12

Satan and his minions know they lack the power to win the souls of men and women by overt warfare, so they use deception and schemes. They lie to all of us. They try to fill our minds with confusion and destructive thoughts. They don't play fair. They use the hurts in dysfunctional families to twist, distort, and crush the hearts of children, and they continue to erect blockages to our growth. We are helpless until we become aware of their plots.

Principle #4—Fortify Yourself With Truth and Love

Study the Scriptures (and encourage your friend or relative to study them) to fortify yourself with the powerful truths of God's Word. Common deceptions focus on shame, fear, confusion, hate, blame, introspection, and denial, but the Bible speaks clearly and powerfully to these issues. The lack of forgiveness seems to be a major strategy that the enemy uses to stunt our growth. But consistent love, honesty, and knowledge of the Scriptures are a powerful combination to promote forgiveness and freedom.

Principle #5—Pray For Wisdom, Insight and Strength

James wrote, *You do not have because you do not ask* (James 4:2). Prayer enables us to tap into the resources of God. We need His wisdom and power to help us fight our battles. Sometimes our prayers can reflect the very deception we are trying to detect and overcome. For example, if we believe that the God we address is harsh or aloof, then our basic concept of God may be the next thing He will change in our growth. For such a fundamental change to take place, we will need to identify our wrong perceptions of God and learn to internalize the truth about Him from the Scripture. Paul wrote:

For though we walk in the flesh, we do not war according to the flesh,
For the weapons of our warfare are not of the flesh, but divinely powerful for the destruction of fortresses.
We are destroying speculations and every lofty thing raised up against the knowledge of God, and we are taking every thought captive to the obedience of Christ.

2 Corinthians 10:3-5

As a person continues to grow in his independence, self-esteem, and healthy relationships, the characteristics of his codependency will gradually subside. Eventually, much of his life will be characterized by new freedom and authentic love in his family and friendships. He will no longer consider himself to be a codependent. He will remember what he has gone through. He will be understanding and compassionate toward those who are in that process themselves. And he will be able to substantially help others conquer their codependency, too.

Helping your friend or relative continue the process of gaining health can be an exciting adventure for him—and for *you*. Probably you both will gain greater insights into the love of God, the freedom, and new motivation you have in Christ, and the perception, love, and separateness you can experience as you grow.

Summary

1. Does your relative or friend understand that "you often have to go down before you can go up"? How can you tell if he understands?

2. Does he understand that "you have to get stronger to go deeper"? How can you tell?

3. Is he harboring bitterness? How can you tell?

4. What can you do to help him experience forgiveness and extend it to those who have hurt him?

5. Do you know the quality and number of relationships he is in?

6. Does he need to develop more healthy relationships? If so, how can you help him?

7. What are evidences of spiritual conflict in his life? In your relationship with him? Have you talked about this with him?

8. How would understanding spiritual conflict help him?

Endnotes

[1] James M. Houston, "The Independence Myth," *Christianity Today* (15 January 1990), p. 32.

[2] Ibid., p. 33.

Chapter 15

Crisis!

Codependent people typically experience all kinds of personal crises. For example, giving all they can give but not being appreciated often causes resentment and leads to a crisis in the relationship with the other unappreciative, rescued person. People who feel controlled may tell the codependent that they can't stand it anymore. The relationship—and the shaky security it afforded—is shattered. The rescuer may then subconsciously neglect certain responsibilities causing a crisis so he can again be the hero by fixing the situation. The "crisis" may not be significant at all. He may blow something out of proportion to make it seem more important. He needs to be needed—the bigger the need, the better. Crises are his cup of tea.

But other crises in a codependent's life are not related to his penchant to rescue, but rather to the process of recovery. These crises have their roots in the overly responsible, controlling, guilt-motivated patterns of codependency, and they may surface at various points in the healing process. We could discuss hundreds of such crises, and a book could be written on each one. But at this point we will only take a brief glance at several of the more common ones. The first two are crises for you, the helper, or counselor. The rest are crises for the codependent.

Crisis: The Codependent Friend or Relative Won't Begin The Process

You may have the purest of intentions to help your friend or relative out of codependency. But he may be stuck in denial...defensive that you would even suggest that he might have a problem...unable or unwilling to even listen to you...or hopeless that there could be any progress.

For some, it's safer not to try to change. Others are so hard and crusty in their denial that they need to have their ground plowed for a while before planting begins. One man was confronted by his employer several times and by those reporting to him on several occasions. He was so skilled at winning loyalty, however, that he fortified himself with the allegiance of other people and chose not to accept the loving reproof he was receiving. He felt abandoned by his employer, but was more sure that he was "right" because of the blind loyalty of those he had won to his cause.

All codependents need (as do the rest of us) time to assimilate reproof. Even in an atmosphere of love and acceptance, the codependent's lack of objectivity makes it hard for him to understand any kind of "criticism." Honesty and openness about your own struggles, coupled with timely and gentle encouragement, provide the best environment for the codependent's insight to begin. Yet the person still may not respond. Then you may want to communicate the consequences of not beginning the healing process. He may perceive what you are saying as a threat, but tell him that it is meant as an encouragement for him to experience real love, peace, and freedom.

Crisis: The Codependent Is One of Your Authority Figures

Ah! This is a thorny problem! What if the rescuer is your spouse, employer, parent, teacher, or some other authority? How do you relate in a healthy way and still be in submission to the person's role?

The first issue is that of control. Submitting to someone does not mean giving up your own identity. It doesn't mean that the other person is in control of you. You have an identity of worth, value, and purpose which makes you a unique and separate person. Parents are to value their children. Husbands are to cherish their wives. Employers are to respect their employees. When this doesn't happen, and when the child, wife, or employee does not feel valued, then perception, love, and separateness need to come from some other legitimate source. We all need to relate to the authorities in our lives in healthy ways.

An employee can work through the situation, or he can leave and get another job, even though that may be difficult. But children and wives do not have that option. They must lean to detach and then decide to find encouragement and value somewhere else. Some people are quick to quote the fifth commandment:

> *"Honor your father and your mother, that your days may be*
> *prolonged in the land which the Lord your God gives you"*
> Exodus 20:12

However, Jesus Christ recognized that a person's commitment to follow Him sometimes brings strife into a family rather than reconciliation.

> *Do not think that I came to bring peace on the earth; I did not come*
> *to bring peace, but a sword,*
> *For I came to set a man against his father, and a daughter against*
> *her mother, and a daughter-in-law against her mother-in-law;*
> *And a man's enemies will be the members of his household.*
> *He who loves father or mother more than Me is not worthy of Me;*
> *and he who loves son or daughter more than Me is not worthy of Me.*
> *And he who does not take his cross and follow after Me is not*
> *worthy of Me.*
> *He who has found his life shall lose it, and he who has lost his life*
> *for My sake shall find it.*
> Matthew 10:34-39

It is very difficult to respond productively to a controlling, rescuing, blaming, manipulative codependent who is in authority over you. The issues are deep and complex, and there are no quick simple solutions. But there *are* some basic principles to follow if you are in this situation:

1. Find a mature person who understands these issues.
2. Develop your own clear perception, and be sure you experience love and separateness.
3. Identify the difficult area—the "flash point"—in the relationship with your codependent authority.

4. Detach and consider your responsibilities in the relationship. The codependent authority probably assumes that your responsibilities should be much higher or much lower than they actually are. Get the advice of a mature, understanding counselor.

5. Decide to communicate the limits of your responsibilities to your authority. Be clear, firm, and kind. If he criticizes you for being "unsubmissive," you may want your mature friend to mediate a discussion between you and your authority to ensure that clear communication takes place.

Keep in mind that even if you detach and respond perfectly, your authority may not be happy with your view of your responsibilities. Do your best to remain patient and loving. Remember that your codependent friend or relative also has a number of crises of his own.

A friend of mine applied these principles in his relationship with his father. Don's father had smothered him with attention, but his approach was harsh and condemning. Nothing Don did ever seemed to be good enough, and Don's father seemed to know about *everything* Don said or did! Don's father told him how to think, how to vote, how to feel, who to date, and how to dress. Don's sense of identity was crushed. He became the person his father said he wanted, even though his dad didn't seem too pleased with the result.

When he was 34, Don started becoming aware of the hurt and anger that had accumulated in his relationship with his father. Don found a support group at his church where he received love, affirmation, and, sometimes, a shocking reality of the truth about his life. He began to develop his own identity and his own ideas. He started making some independent choices even though he knew his father wouldn't like them—such as wearing more modern clothes. He had always wanted to change the preppy look his father demanded that he wear. So of all the many, many areas where Don needed to express his new identity, he decided to use the clothes issue to take his first stand. Don realized that his new style of clothes would create a big flap when his father saw him, so he carefully considered how to respond to his dad's attacks.

As Don drove across town to his father's house, he began to panic. *I don't think I can go through with this!* he thought, but then he remembered some affirming statements made by people in his support group. He thought, *I'm 34 years old, not*

5! If I want to wear these clothes, I can wear them. I can act like an adult and take responsibility for my own life whether my father treats me like an adult or not!

When he walked in the front door of his dad's house, he received a long stare but his father didn't say anything about his clothes. *Maybe I've only imagined that Dad is manipulative and demanding*, Don considered. But after an hour or so, his father said, "Are all of your good clothes dirty?"

OK, here we go, thought Don. He explained that his tastes in fashion had changed, and that he was wearing some different kinds of clothes. His father bristled, "You look like an idiot! I don't want *my son* wearing clothes like that!"

With all the composure he could muster, Don explained that he was 34 years old and capable of making his own decisions. He said, "I hope you'll respect my opinions and my choices. You may not always like them, but I hope you'll agree with my right to make them."

Don's father didn't like Don's new identity or new freedom at all, but Don did. Over the next several months, Don continued to learn and grow in his new identity. He tried to be sure to respect his father, but he realized that he was not responsible to do everything his father wanted just to please him.

Crisis: Deeper Issues Surface

As a person begins the process of recovery from codependency, deeper issues often surface. One young lady admitted having an eating disorder for years. A gentleman confessed to abusing prescription drugs because the pain had gotten so bad. A man confided that he was contemplating suicide. A lady wept as she told how she had been sexually abused as a child by her uncle and cousins. A young man described his involvement with the occult before he became a believer, and told of experiencing terrible nightmares and uncontrollable urges for years. A college student described being manipulated to help his mother because she threatened to kill herself if he didn't. A woman in our church told me that her father regularly beat her mother and abused her brother.

You can provide a wonderful environment of love and acceptance for codependents beginning the healing process. These people wouldn't tell you such things if they didn't feel safe with you. But recognize when you are in over your head. When someone has a problem or a set of problems that is more than you can handle, direct him to get professional help from a trained, biblically-based Christian counselor. You don't have to solve all his deepest problems. It is enough that you are a conduit to get him the kind of help he needs.

Crisis: Complicating Factors Confuse and Inhibit Progress

Financial problems, difficulties at work or school, problems with a spouse or children, physical problems caused by stress, or other sources or any of a myriad of other factors can complicate and confuse a person trying to deal with codependency. Sometimes he may intentionally use these as a smoke screen to avoid dealing with his problems. "I don't have time to focus on myself right now," he might say. "I'm too busy doing my job. I'm too tired when I get home." Or, "You don't understand. She really needs me right now. What would she do if I didn't help her?"

Often, however, these problems are *not* smoke screens. They are very real, and they pose genuine problems for a person trying to work through the recovery process. He needs help to sort out the issues logically and carefully.

You can help by letting him know that he is not alone in this process. Take him step by step, decision by decision, until he gets his head above water. His problems often occur because someone else has been irresponsible and has expected to be rescued by him. By helping him take responsibility for his own decisions while letting other people live with the consequences of their irresponsibility, he can make progress.

This separation of responsibilities can be very awkward at times. In some cases the person might even need to separate portions of the family budget so an irresponsible alcoholic or addict can't throw away the money meant for groceries or the children's clothes. This kind of issue is very real and is no minor problem. If you determine that these problems are not a smoke screen by your friend or relative, you may want to get the advice of someone who has helped several other people through similar severe problems.

Crisis: The Codependent Is Overwhelmed
By the Reality of Pain and Anger

When the cap comes off the cesspool of repressed emotions, the resulting feelings can plunge someone into the pits of despair or into raging anger. He may realize that he has feared rejection all his life. And he can become overwhelmed by the stark reality of what has happened, who has hurt him, the tragic consequences, and his own negative impact on others because of the dysfunction in his life.

This can be a very difficult point for you and for your friend or relative. He may be out of control in his anger. Help him understand that he is feeling the backlog of years of anger. The anger is real. It is understandable. It should not be repressed, but it does need to be controlled to some degree so the person won't do something he will regret later. Relate to him how the shock of reality affected you, and how wide swings of emotions are a normal response at first.

The overwhelming emotions may produce depression, which probably stems from a deep sense of loss about his life. If so, offer comfort and encouragement. Let him know you won't leave him alone. Give him time to grieve, because he has indeed suffered great loss.

Again, if the person's reaction is unmanageable or if he doesn't experience some degree of comfort after a while, seek professional help.

Crisis: The Person Overreacts and
Goes From Rescuing To Rebellion

When you take the initiative to lovingly confront your friend or relative, he may assume that you are attacking him. He may go one step farther and include you among the ones who have hurt him most deeply. He may blame you for his problems.

Not all of his anger and rebellion will be focused toward you personally. Much of it is an overreaction to the feeling of being controlled and manipulated. He determines, "I'm not going to let *anybody* ever control me again! I'm not going to let *anybody* tell me what to do!" For a while, he may be quite out of control, disregarding or disobeying any and all forms of authority (such as work, school, speed limits, church, parents, and any others).

Talk to him about the swing in his response from rescuing to rebellion. Be honest and calm, but be firm. If he attacks or blames you, tell him how you feel about it. It is also a good idea to tell him the consequences of his behavior if he keeps it up—how it will affect his relationship with you as well as every area of his life in which he is overreacting. Some overreaction is normal and expected, but extreme cases need to be addressed firmly and lovingly.

Crisis: A Counselor or Friend Advises Divorce

Several months ago a man called me. He explained that he and his wife had been going to a counselor for therapy concerning their codependency. After several sessions, the counselor had advised this man's wife to divorce him. "What can I do?" he lamented.

Codependents need to detach, but divorce as a remedy is much too extreme. Codependents often think that the problem in the relationship is with the spouse. Then, divorce seems like an attractive option to escape the problem. The real problem, however, continues into the next relationship (and the next and...) if the underlying problems of control, rescuing, denial, hurt, anger, and guilt are not resolved. The goal of detaching is to provide the opportunity to reflect and make good healthy decisions. The goal in a strained relationship is reconciliation. This comes through perception, love, and healthy separateness—not escape.

In relationships with a spouse or children, encourage the codependent to detach emotionally, and maybe get away for a few days from time to time to get a clearer perspective. Separation can be a very healthy—and very loving—way to detach. It allows both people to experience counseling, healing, and hope for themselves and the relationship. Codependents tend to cling to the one who is hurting them, even physically abusing them. They are so afraid of being alone that separation allows enough distance to allow the constant pressure and habits in the relationship to subside. Later, when healing is well under way, the two can be reunited.

Separation can be a very positive step in some relationships. Long-term separation may be considered in extreme circumstances where abuse is present. In some cases, separation fails to produce the desired results, and reconciliation is not possible. When persistent physical abuse, severe emotional abuse or child molestation exist in a family, it is an untenable situation for the spouse and the children. In such cases, a permanent separation may be the only choice. Divorce is never a preferable option, but sometimes it may be the least bad of all the alternatives.

This is indeed an emotional and controversial issue. Pastors, scholars, counselors, and laypeople differ widely in their views of what the Bible teaches on divorce. It is not in the scope of this book to outline the various positions authorities take on these subjects. But I do believe it is worthwhile for a codependent to consider separation—whether for a short time or a long time—as a healthy means of detachment so healing can occur for the individual and his family.

Describe the goal of detaching to your friend or relative. Help him see that its purpose is not escape but health and reconciliation. If he refuses to listen, take another friend with you to talk things through and plead with him not to divorce. Sometimes a third person can bring reason where there was none. Also, throughout this process, discuss the hurt and anger that has precipitated the desire to escape through divorce.

Crisis: Family Members Try To Force the Codependent To Return To His Old Role of Rescuer

Family members rarely applaud when a rescuer stops rescuing. They want him to continue. If *he* stops, who will take care of them? His personal growth and independence is a threat to the system established in the dysfunctional family. This pressure to revert to old patterns of behavior may take the form of subtle passive-aggressive manipulation, or it may be through outright condemnation and ridicule. "How could you be so selfish? You *never* think about us!" That kind of manipulation has worked wonders in the past. Will it work now to cause the codependent to postpone his healing process and force him to rescue again?

Pressure to continue rescuing is very common in dysfunctional families, so try to prepare your friend or relative for it before it happens. He may not believe you. (His lack of objectivity about his family may not be conquered yet.)

When the pressure to rescue *does* begin, you may want to talk about genuine love. Ask him questions like: How do people treat each other when they love each other? Do the members of your family value you and respect your separateness? How would they treat you if they genuinely loved you?

Discussions about these questions may help the other person realize that he may never be loved by them the way he wants to be loved. And this realization may propel him beyond the bargaining stage.

Summary

A codependent faces many crises in life. Some he creates. Some are created by others. Some are imaginary. Some are very real. Some affect the people who are trying to help him. Challenge him to take the next step to work through each crisis, and help him grow in his perception, love, and separateness.

1.   Which of these crises affects your friend or relative? Which one(s) affect you?

2.   What are some specific steps that you need to take? What steps does the codependent person need to take? What steps do others need to take?

3.   Discuss each of these crises listed in this chapter with your codependent friend or relative. In each case, ask him, "How does this apply to you?"

Chapter 16

Authentic Christianity

If the topic of codependency is new to you, it would not be unusual for you to have questions at this point—perhaps even doubts. While this book should have answered many of your concerns about the nature of codependency, you may be asking yourself things like: Is all this stuff about codependency just narcissism? Isn't it a self-indulgent preoccupation? Is it just a good excuse to condone selfishness?

No. Codependency is a real problem in millions of lives. It stems from the deep hurts caused by neglect, anger, denial, addictions, and emotional wounds which occur in some families.

John Calvin was a 16th century scholar, theologian, and cornerstone figure of the Protestant Reformation. He wrote, "Without knowledge of self there is no knowledge of God."[1] He further explained, "The purpose of the knowledge of ourselves is not that we would love ourselves. Instead knowledge of ourselves reveals our need for God and our need to experience His love, forgiveness, and strength."[2] The more we experience all God has to offer, the more we can then make choices to "give up our lives" (Matthew 16:24-26; Luke 14:25-27, et al) and devote ourselves to godly sacrifice, stewardship, obedience, and commitment. The process of being Christ's disciple builds strength and stability. It comes through internal change, and it revolutionizes our identity, values, motives, and actions.

How is such strength developed? How do these wonderful changes occur? The first step is being honest about the hurts and blockages that hinder our growth. Healing is necessary before real strength can be developed.

A person who becomes aware of accumulated hurts becomes self-absorbed for a while. This should not seem unusual because his healing will require time and attention. It doesn't happen by osmosis. A person with a broken leg needs to go to a doctor, get X-rays, see if surgery is necessary, and have a cast put on. At that point, the pain will immobilize the person, usually for days if not longer. But after a while he becomes more mobile. He is more productive. He becomes less preoccupied with his leg.

After a few months, the cast is taken off and he can begin to rehabilitate the atrophied leg muscles. Additional months later, the leg may be fit for a jog around the block. Is the time and attention required for the broken leg to heal selfish or narcissistic? No. It is reasonable.

A codependent's initial preoccupation with his own life is not the ultimate goal of healing. It is only the first stage in a process that will lead to a strong sense of biblical identity, genuine love, and selfless service. And these things are all components of authentic Christianity. The healing process begins and continues with the person's growing sense of reality about life. Denial begins to erode as he becomes more aware of his sins and the sins of others against him. Then, he can increasingly experience forgiveness for his wrongs and comfort for the hurts he has endured.

His view of God changes. Where once God seemed aloof or cruel, He is now perceived as a just and merciful Father. His black-or-white outlook on life blends into more greys as he becomes more comfortable with the many ambiguities of each day. He develops more authentic relationships, increasingly based on honest communication, respect for each person's separateness, and genuine love.

I have watched many people at the turning points in this process. It is always a delight to see someone muster the courage to take the next step—even though he might be scared to death! But it also sad to see others so frightened, hardened, bitter, or blind that they refuse to take the next step—or even the first step.

The healing process involves an interplay of spiritual, relational, physical, and emotional factors. In our culture, we try to categorize, analyze, and segment these factors so that we can fix each one with quick, easy answers. But the codependent must realize that they are inextricably related.

The intense drive to rescue, for example, has its roots in emotional pain stemming from strained relationships which distort a person's view of God and often result in a variety of stress-related physical ailments (gastrointestinal problems, tension headaches, the lethargy of depression, etc.). If only the surface symptoms of this deeply rooted problem are addressed, the person may experience temporary relief. But the roots are still there and will typically create the full, combined, negative impact again before too long.

For example, one gentleman was treated symptomatically by an internist for chronic diarrhea, but the stresses in his life from a dependent and controlling wife remained hidden from the doctor. A woman came for counseling and she complained of feeling very lonely and hurt, but she avoided any discussion of her relationships with her parents, brothers, or husband. Somehow, she wanted to resolve her emotional pain apart from relational reality.

Quite often, people live for years with a distorted view of God and remain unaware of their misperceptions. They read the Scriptures through distorted lenses unaware of any problem. Their erroneous interpretation of the Bible only reinforces their perception that God is cruel, demanding, or aloof. They seldom if ever consider the possibility that their view of God and their self-concept have been shaped by their codependent relationship with their parents.

Addressing the root issues of codependency in the context of the spiritual, emotional, physical, and relational factors will take more time and attention than the quick-fix approach. It can't be rushed. And while it may be more complicated, it does, however, offer more hope for genuine progress.

The slow and painful process of addressing these root issues affects the most fundamental motivations of a codependent—or anyone else, for that matter. Instead of rescuing, giving, and serving in order to be appreciated and affirmed, the person's growing strength and stability make it possible to love and give with an open hand, not demanding an appreciative response. Luke referred to this selfless motivation in his account of Jesus' sermon on the Mount:

And if you love those who love you, what credit is that to you? For even sinners love those who love them.

*And if you do good to those who do good to you, what credit is that
to you? For even sinners do the same.*

*And if you lend to those from whom you expect to receive,
what credit is that to you? Even sinners lend to sinners, in order to
receive back the same amount.*

*But love your enemies, and do good, and lend, expecting nothing
in return; and your reward will be great, and you will be sons of the
Most High; for He Himself is kind to ungrateful and evil men.*

Be merciful, just as your Father is merciful.

*And do not judge and you will not be judged; and do not condemn,
and you will not be condemned; pardon, and you will be pardoned.*

Luke 6:32-37

Codependents tend to interpret the admonition to avoid judging (v. 37) as an excuse to keep from dealing with reality. "No," one woman told me, "I shouldn't even think about my father's alcoholism. That would be judging him, and that's wrong!" And they tend to view positive actions such as loving, doing good, and lending as cardinal virtues without analyzing the deeper motivation that Jesus talks about. They lack the motives ("expecting nothing in return") and the strength of character that true service requires.

Scripture commands believers to try to please other people, but the context of the instruction also makes the motivation clear. We are to serve others for *their* good, not so *we* will receive appreciation. We must be careful to avoid the idolatry of pleasing people so they will, in return, give us the love we want. The contrast between this kind of idolatry and pure service is seen clearly when we compare Galatians 1:10 with Romans 15:2.

*For am I now seeking the favor of men, or of God? Or am I striving
to please men? If I were still trying to please men, I would not be a bondservant of Christ.*

Galatians 1:10

Let each of us please his neighbor for his good, to his edification.

Romans 15:2

Genuine recovery from codependency does not make a person self-indulgent or obnoxious. Far from that, the process of growing secure in his new identity and forming healthy relationships provides strength and godly character. He becomes able to love, give, and serve without all the twisted motives and deception so common in codependency.

Here are some changes that will take place as this progress occurs:

- Instead of a lack of objectivity, he develops a clearer perception of God, himself, and other people.
- Instead of a warped sense of responsibility, he understands he is accountable only within certain limits. He gives because he wants to instead of feeling as if he has to.
- Instead of being easily controlled by others, he has more of a sense of strength and identity. He values his own feelings, thoughts, and decisions.
- Instead of controlling others, he values them enough to let them make their own decisions.
- Instead of continuing to repress hurt and anger, he is honest about his feelings and deals with them appropriately.
- Instead of feeling recurring guilt and shame, he experiences more forgiveness, peace, and contentment.
- Instead of loneliness, he develops authentic relationships based on honesty, respect, and love.

Many of us have taken various vocational tests to help us determine our strengths, weaknesses, and job fit. These tests, however, generally reflect emotional abnormalities more than true personality. Most of us don't know what we're really like because our lives have been clouded and compelled by our thirst for approval and recognition.

Several years ago I took a test that showed that I was "very goal-oriented, but given to swings of emotion and perspective." (Knowing what I do now, I would interpret those comments as "driven" and seeing everything as "black or white!") The test also showed that I valued other people's approval of me very highly and was "malleable under pressure." (That means "easily manipulated!") Recently, I took the same test again to see if all I have been learning about codependency has changed my life very much. I was encouraged! This test showed that I wasn't nearly as goal-oriented (driven) as before, much more stable (instead of black and white), and not nearly so easily swayed by others' opinions of me. I'm growing! I've got a long way to go, but at least I'm on the road.

This growth process frees a person from the oppressive bondage of hurt, bitterness, shame, and manipulation so he can live more wholeheartedly for Christ. A deep experience of the love of God has a powerful, liberating, and motivating influence:

> *For the love of Christ controls us, having concluded this, that one died for all, therefore all died;*
> *And He died for all, that they who live should no longer live for themselves, but for Him who died and rose again on their behalf.*
> 2 Corinthians 5:14-15

Authentic Christianity. Changed lives. Is this possible? Yes! Is it attractive? Yes, very attractive! The reason people were so attracted to Christ—and the reason the religious establishment was so threatened by Him—was that Jesus was honest about the real issues in people's lives. He didn't mince words. He didn't offer superficial solutions and quick fixes. He offered lasting solutions: authentic love, forgiveness, and acceptance to meet deep needs.

As individuals become honest about their needs and experience—genuinely experience—the life-changing love and power of God in their hearts and relationships, other needy people throughout the world will see that help is available and flock to Christ. People will experience deep healing of their pain. They will repent from sins of bitterness. Relationships will be restored. And an awakening will break out as God's Spirit works in countless lives.

Codependency is a problem of extremes when what we need is balance. We need *both* separateness and intimacy, not one or the other. Finding that balance is extremely difficult without someone to help provide perception and encouragement. Codependents need someone who will allow them to take the risk of being themselves. If that person doesn't condemn them or leave them, they may have the courage to take that risk again. Slowly, cautiously, painfully, the threat of rejection and condemnation is replaced by a new identity and confidence—the ability to be both separate and loving. That's real health!

A few weeks ago I talked to a middle-aged friend who is growing in his perceptions and learning to experience genuine love and separateness. He said, "I wish I had learned all this a lot earlier in my life. It sure would have prevented a lot of pain—for myself, my wife, and my children. But God has done so much during the past year or so. I'm very grateful! Learning this is better now than later—and it's a lot better now than not at all!"

Your codependent friend or relative may feel a sense of loss for not dealing with these issues earlier in his life, but he will be glad to discover the freedom and love he can experience now. The process is hard, but it's worth it. It starts by someone having the courage to be honest with one other person.

Summary

1. Describe "authentic Christianity."

2. How have your seen your friend or relative change during the process so far regarding his perception, love, and separateness?

3.   What are the obstacles to his or her growth at this point?

4.   What is the next step for him or her?

Endnotes

[1]   John Calvin, *Institute of the Christian Religion* vol. I., translated by Ford
     Lewis Battles, The Library of Christian Classics (Philadelphia, PA: The
     Westminster Press, 1960).

[2]   *Ibid.*, vol. XX, 35-37.

Bibliography

Armand, Nicholi. "Changes in the American Family: Their Impact on Individual Development and on Society." *Family Research Council*. Reprint.

Brophy, Beth. "Children Under Stress." *U.S. News & World Report*, October 27, 1986.

Calvin, John. *Institute of the Christian Religion*. vol. I. translated by Ford Lewis Battles, The Library of Christian Classics. Philadelphia, PA: The Westminster Press, 1960.

Calvin, John. *Institute of the Christian Religion*. vol. XX. translated by Ford Lewis Battles, The Library of Christian Classics. Philadelphia, PA: The Westminster Press, 1960.

Casale, Anthony M. USA Today, *Tracking Tomorrow's Trends*. Kansas City: Andrews, McMeel, and Parker, 1986.

Crabb, Larry. *Inside Out*. Colorado Springs, CO: NavPress, 1988.

Houston, James M. "The Independence Myth." *Christianity Today*, January 15, 1990.

Kleinmuntz, Benjamin. *Essentials of Abnormal Psychology*. 2nd ed. San Francisco: Harper and Row, 1980.

McGee, Robert, Jim Craddock, and Pat Springle. *Your Parents and You*. Dallas, TX: Rapha Publishing/Word, Inc., 1990.

Springle, Pat. *Codependency*. Houston and Dallas, TX: Rapha Publishing/Word, Inc., 1990.

Steiner, Claude M. *Scripts People Live*. New York: Grove Press, 1974.

Stephen Series Leader's Manual. St. Louis, MO: Stephen Ministries, 1983.

Team Building Seminar. Minneapolis, MN: Campus Crusade for Christ, 1987.

Wallerstein, Judith S. "Bouncing Back Slowly." *New York Times*, January 22, 1989.

Wegscheider-Cruse, Sharon. *Choicemaking*. Deerfield Beach, FL: Health Communications, 1985.

Wegscheider-Cruse, Sharon. *The Family Trap*.

White, Burton. *The First Three Years of Life*. rev. ed. New York: Prentice-Hall Press, 1985.